E-COACHING

In a rapidly moving world where so many of our day-to-day activities are now online, it has become essential to adapt coaching processes in order to better suit clients' circumstances and needs. Above all, clients want sustainable and time-efficient results. Electronic coaching (e-coaching) is an inevitable development for every professional who coaches, mentors, teaches, supervises, guides or helps people in their jobs.

The book is underpinned by a theoretical framework that introduces a new model of people development (the ABC model), inspired by Graham Alexander's GROW model, and a new text-based coaching method inspired by Brown and Levinson's politeness theory. *E-coaching* is practical in its approach, with explanations on safeguarding the security and privacy of your clients, how to calculate rates, managing expectations and other important aspects of coaching online.

The first English-language text available on e-coaching, this book presents a unique combined approach of method and technique, supplemented with a sample e-coaching programme. It is a must-read for all coaches, mentors, supervisors, teachers or HR professionals who want to coach in a modern way, as well as students studying on coaching courses.

Anne Ribbers is a researcher in the field of coaching at the Department of Human Resource Studies, Tilburg University, the Netherlands. She is a psychology graduate from Tilburg University and Columbia University, co-founder of eCoachPro (www.ecoachpro.org) and the editor of the European Mentoring & Coaching Council's *International Journal of Mentoring and Coaching*.

Alexander Waringa is a social psychologist and certified e-coach. He is co-founder of eCoachPro (www.ecoachpro.org) and a board member of the European Mentoring & Coaching Council, the Netherlands. He is Ambassador of eHealth at the Dutch Association of Psychologists and currently completing his Ph.D. research on the effectiveness of e-coaching at Tilburg University, the Netherlands.

E-COACHING

Theory and practice for a new online approach to coaching

Anne Ribbers and Alexander Waringa

Routledge
Taylor & Francis Group

LONDON AND NEW YORK

First published 2012
by Uitgeverij Boom Nelissen, Amsterdam

English language edition 2015
by Routledge
2 Park Square, Milton Park, Abingdon, Oxon OX14 4RN

and by Routledge
711 Third Avenue, New York, NY 10017

Routledge is an imprint of the Taylor & Francis Group, an informa business

British Library Cataloguing in Publication Data
A catalogue record for this book is available from the British Library

Library of Congress Cataloging in Publication Data
Ribbers, Anne.
[E-coaching. English]
E-coaching : theory and practice for a new online approach to coaching /
Anne Ribbers and Alexander Waringa.
pages cm.
"First published 2012 by Uitgeverij Boom Nelissen, Amsterdam."
Includes bibliographical references and index.
1. Personal coaching. 2. Telematics. 3. Internet in psychotherapy.
I. Waringa, Alexander. II. Title.
BF637.P36R5313 2015
158.3—dc23
2014036636

ISBN: 978-1-138-77873-3 (hbk)
ISBN: 978-1-138-77874-0 (pbk)
ISBN: 978-1-315-77167-0 (ebk)

Typeset in Bembo
by FiSH Books Ltd, Enfield

CONTENTS

IILLUSTRATIONS

Figures

Table

FOREWORD

Language is what connects us, and coaches know this better than anyone. It is one of the most essential tools in the coaching profession, and we use it every day. With this powerful tool, we can carefully shape the coaching dialogue and the coach–client relationship. The essential click between coach and client can only be realized once the two parties feel they are speaking the same language.

As young children, we both learned the vital importance of speaking the same language when our families moved to countries where our mother tongue was entirely foreign. By mastering these new languages as soon as possible, we were able to connect with the people around us. We later learned the scientific principles of this process during social psychology lectures given by Prof. John Rijsman (this was also where we met and started working together) at Tilburg University. Prof. Rijsman introduced us to the world of social constructionism. This philosophical theory asserts there is no such thing as a uniform objective reality. In dialogue and interaction with other individuals reality is created. Establishing a common language and mutually agreeing upon the meaning and interpretation of words create shared realities. Take the word 'love', for example. By agreeing on a common understanding of the word 'love', we can determine its nature, put it in context and give it substance. The words contained in each language allow its speakers to create and define a communal reality.

The effect of this principle is wonderfully illustrated in George Orwell's novel *1984*. It describes how a totalitarian state diminishes its citizens' everyday subjective realities by systematically limiting the number of words available to express particular thoughts, ideas and emotions. Each new edition of the dictionary of Newspeak – the state-sanctioned language – contains fewer words than its predecessor. The reasoning behind this is that if the words do not exist, the thoughts and feelings that corresponded to them can no longer be expressed and will simply wither and die. In this way, the state imposes its reality on its subjects, who are no longer able to voice any alternative realities.

The world depicted in *1984* would have no place for coaches. 'Newspeak' would paralyze us, as its purpose is entirely contradictory to the basic principle of coaching, i.e. to help the client express their inner thoughts, emotions, insights, answers and solutions.

Another aspect of *1984* is the omnipresence of technical communication media. The totalitarian state uses this technology to exert maximum control over its subjects ('Big Brother is watching you!'). Although we may not realize it sometimes, we live in an age in which electronic communication equipment is all around us every second of every day. Thankfully, in our culture, this technology is used to a limited extent as a method of controlling the populace. The wide variety of available media is used to share and exchange information and to communicate in the easiest and most convenient way possible. Boundaries are fading and physical distances are overcome by the unlimited possibilities of a wide variety of online media. Coaches use language to collaboratively shape a relevant reality together with their clients. By combining this mission statement with modern communication media, we believe a whole new world of opportunities can be opened up in the field of coaching. Our e-coaching methods and models are built upon this fundamental belief and this book offers us the perfect opportunity to share these insights with you.

Co-creation was a vital factor in writing this book, as we worked together with a huge number of experts in the field to develop a new, ready-to-use online coaching medium. Without the tireless contribution of all of these people, we couldn't possibly have written this book. Particular thanks go out to the following people: Stephanie Bode, for the vast quantity of preparatory work she contributed; Marjanne Peters, a trainer in our education programs who gave us the benefit of her extensive knowledge while fine-tuning the eCP method; Lidwien Kamp, whose enthusiasm convinced her coaches to adopt our e-coaching methods; Marcel Herwegh, who drew upon all of his experience as an e-coach to provide a fantastic example of a full e-coaching program; Lia Ribbers and Marieke Schipper for their contribution to the original version of this book; Sabrina Gomersall for her native English support with some difficult terminology; Suzanne Van Groos for her enthusiastic support in realizing our English manuscript; and all of the coaches/e-coaches who were willing to share their realities with us during the writing process Finally, we would of course like to thank both of our families, who provide us with an invaluable and inexhaustible source of inspiration, support and love.

The ethos of this book is that by working together, you can create a workable and pleasant reality. We hope the book will help you incorporate this principle into your daily online coaching practice. We wish you a pleasant and enlightening read!

Anne Ribbers and Alexander Waringa
April 2015

PART I

Introduction to the world of e-coaching

Electronic coaching, or e-coaching for short, is a new branch of coaching that is rapidly gaining popularity. In Part I of this book, we will explain the relevant theory behind the field e-coaching and how the discipline came into being. We will also talk about the various possible applications of e-coaching. We then go into greater detail, discussing the underlying processes involved in e-coaching from both a client and coach perspective. In order to fully comprehend the concept of e-coaching, it is important to gain insight into these specific psychological and psycho linguistic processes and the dynamics involved especially for text-based coaching. In our experience, most coaches that try e-coaching without proper preparation tend to throw in the towel quickly. This happens because they communicate with their e-coachees in the same way as they do during face-to-face (F2F) coaching. For this reason, we will discuss the advantages and disadvantages of online communication. Subsequently, we will introduce the ABC model, which stands for Accelerated Behavioural Change. This model is specifically developed for online facilitation of behavioural change. To close Part I of the book, we will introduce the eCoachPro (eCP) method for text-based e-coaching and discuss a number of theories upon which it is based. We developed this method ourselves in order to ensure that online communication within e-coaching programmes is conducted effectively and efficiently.

In Part II, we describe the practical application of the ABC model and the eCP method. We also provide a summary of all of the essential preconditions for successful e-coaching programmes. Part III then perfectly combines the theory from Part I and the practical application from Part II in the form of a comprehensive example of a real-life e-coaching programme.

1

E-COACHING

The new world of online coaching

The Internet phenomenon is here to stay. Around the world, there are nearly three billion Internet users, which is approaching half of the world's population. We live in a rapidly changing world with more and more being demanded of both our cognitive and social skills. For the generation born within the last ten years, clicking a mouse or tapping a touchscreen is as natural as breathing or blinking. Internet via the World Wide Web is almost limitlessly accessible and creates opportunities that have been available to no other generation in history. The Internet not only satisfies an increasing demand for information, it also creates a wealth of opportunities for entertainment, social contact, communication and interaction.

Technology is the driving force behind this rapidly changing environment. However, due to the increasing complexity of the world we live in, there is a risk that we will be expected to absorb and process more information than the human brain can possibly handle. This problem demands that new applications are developed to provide order and structure, reducing the complexity to manageable levels. Innovative concepts such as e-coaching can help people to adapt to the constant change of our increasingly complex world. Until now, e-coaching has mainly been associated with speed, availability and accessibility: support at the click of a mouse. This viewpoint mainly focuses on the benefits and opportunities offered by technology and the Internet. However, the opportunities for intra- and interpersonal processes get far less airtime. It is in these intra-personal and interpersonal processes where the true benefit of e-coaching lies. In this chapter, we will explain the various aspects of e-coaching and introduce a new definition of e-coaching. To close the chapter, we will give a number of reasons why you should embrace this innovative coaching approach.

1.1 Existing forms of online learning/coaching

Although coaching is practiced on an enormous scale, there is few empirical data on why it works; about the active ingredients. Very little – if any – scientific research has been conducted into e-coaching. However, research is available about various other successful forms of online guidance. For this reason, we have examined how much overlap there is between e-coaching and two other online guidance methods: e-learning and e-therapy.

1.1.1 E-learning

No matter which of the various definitions of coaching you subscribe to, one aspect is always prevalent: the facilitation of learning. Learning is an essential part of the coaching process. Online learning is also known as e-learning, and can be described as the provision of educational programmes or training by means of various electronic media such as the Internet, intranet, extranet, audio–visual devices, VIOP (Voice over Internet) and/or CD-ROMs. For this type of education, technology is used to enrich the lessons and learning experiences. By using online media, you can create a virtual learning environment that provides information over the Internet. It also facilitates new applications for the data and in-depth investigation of specific information, which offer fantastic new insights. As with the analogue variety, the main goal of online learning is to gain new knowledge. Within the field of coaching, learning new information is an instrumental factor in achieving specific behavioural change.

1.1.2 E-therapy

The term e-therapy encompasses all forms of remote therapy conducted using technology. There are many different forms, such as e-health and e-counselling. Despite the widespread use of e-therapy, there is still no absolute definition. In our opinion, the American National Board for Certified Counselors (NBCC) gives a useful definition. Although this definition relates to e-counselling, it can easily be used to define e-therapy in the broadest possible sense of the term. Their definition is as follows: 'Internet counseling involves asynchronous and synchronous remote interaction among counselors and clients using e-mail, chat, and videoconferencing features of the Internet to communicate.' This definition includes another aspect in addition to the use of ICT, i.e. that it involves remote interaction. In other words, it states that you can offer therapy that is potentially time and location independent.

It is no coincidence that e-therapy is popular with clients both young and old. Various studies have shown that e-therapy is extremely effective in treating psychological conditions such as depression, anxiety and trauma. Further research has shown that online therapy is also effective for conditions such as asthma or chronic fatigue syndrome, and a recent study showed that online therapy helps to lower patients' blood pressure. Pilot studies have also been conducted that compare in-person therapy and e-therapy. The initial results show that e-therapy can be just as effective, and in some situations, even more effective than regular therapy. One of the important advantages of e-therapy is its accessibility, as communication can be conducted remotely and with a large degree of anonymity.

E-therapy can be seen as a technological response to society's demand for care that is unrestricted by geographical, physical, psychological and/or financial obstacles. It makes care more accessible for groups such as young people, people in full-time employment, the hard of hearing, lonely and isolated people or housebound people. Anyone with an Internet connection can gain access to e-therapy.

1.1.3 Similarities and differences

Although e-coaching does have a degree of overlap with e-learning and e-therapy, there are a number of fundamental differences. In general, e-therapy is conducted via supply-driven programmes with a modular set-up. Often, it consists of self-help books and programmes that have been adapted for online usage. It involves therapies and programmes that are mainly protocol-based, with the client completing a number of standard modules and conducting sporadic online contact with a professional. Important aspects of e-therapy include psychoeducation,[1] written assignments, behavioural experiments and homework. These types of programme involve weekly online contact with a psychologist or therapist. Research shows that a large amount of personal online contact greatly benefits the effectiveness of the treatment.

Coaching is rarely supply-driven, protocols are infrequently used and personal contact is of essential importance to the nature and structure of the process. Every coaching objective is unique, personal and requires a made-to-measure approach. Furthermore, the central aspect of coaching is the dialogue. During the dialogue, the client is confronted with the coaching issue by means of questions, reflection exercises and introspection. To compare e-coaching with e-therapy, it is best to look at e-therapy programmes that involve interpersonal contact. E-coaching and e-therapy both involve written exercises, behavioural experiments and knowledge transfer. Due to this overlap, we can learn a lot about e-coaching from the research into e-therapy and the experiences of those that practice it.

1.2 Definition of e-coaching

E-coaching is also known as online coaching, remote coaching, web coaching, cyber coaching, digital coaching, i-coaching, distance coaching and virtual coaching. There are also other types in which specific software is used, such as chat coaching (via a chat program), video coaching (using a webcam), SMS coaching (via text messages) and Skype coaching (combination of Voice over Internet (VIOP) and webcam). The authoritative *Handbook of the Psychology of Coaching and Mentoring* edited by psychologist Jonathan Passmore and colleagues includes one chapter on 'virtual coaching'. In this chapter several interesting examples of e-coaching are described, including a variety of definitions. Top coach and leadership expert David Clutterbuck (2010, co-founder of the European Mentoring and Coaching Council) defined e-coaching as a *developmental partnership in which the learning dialogue is conducted online.*

Based on this definition and the overlap between e-therapy and e-learning described in Section 1.1.3, we have formulated a more specific definition of e-coaching:

> *E-coaching is a non-hierarchical developmental partnership between two parties separated by a geographical distance, in which the learning and reflection process is conducted via both analogue and virtual means.*

This definition is made up of three key aspects:

1 Coaching is involved. The lack of a hierarchical and advisory relationship is characteristic of e-coaching, which intrinsically distinguishes it from e-learning and e-therapy.
2 The learning and reflection process is conducted both in a practical setting (on the job) and in the client's everyday environment (analogue). This learning and reflection process is facilitated by using the Internet (digital). This approach enables the client to practice new skills in relevant real-life situations.
3 Communication between the coach and client is not conducted in close proximity (in person), but at a distance (remote). Furthermore, in the case of email coaching each party decides when to read the messages sent to them (asynchronous). As a result, the coaching programme is both time and location independent.

1.3 E-coaching and coaching: similarities and differences

Remote one-on-one interaction is the central aspect of e-coaching, with little to no direct contact, i.e. face-to-face (F2F) coaching. The goal of both e-coaching and traditional F2F coaching is to provide effective personal guidance to induce the desired behavioural change, hopefully resulting in the client achieving his/her primary objectives. Coaching enables clients to improve their knowledge, skills and competencies and apply these new abilities in their everyday life. One of the most famous researchers in our field is the coaching psychologist Anthony Grant, who has formulated six essential steps in the coaching process based on recent research into the application of solution focused, appreciative and cognitive behavioural coaching, in addition to the discipline of 'positive psychology'. These six steps can be used to realize any coaching objective that a client wants to achieve:

1 Identify the desired result.
2 Set specific goals.

3   Boost motivation by identifying strengths and building self-confidence.
4   Identify available tools and formulate specific action plans.
5   Monitor and evaluate progress until goals are achieved.
6   Adjust the action plans based on feedback.

The last two steps are known as a self-regulating cycle in which the monitoring, evaluation and adjustment initiate a process of learning by self-reflection. In the field of e-coaching, the emphasis is on steps 3 and 4. This enables acceleration of the coaching process, which in turn gets the client to truly internalize what they have learned. As a result, it is possible to achieve more enduring results with e-coaching in a shorter space of time. This principle is explained in greater detail in Chapter 5: The ABC model for actual change.

1.4 Practical reasons to get started with e-coaching

Online generation

Today's society is undergoing a boom in online technology, resulting in a growing need to work online. The average person spends 23.8 hours online every month. For example in North America people spend 37.2 hours online versus Europe with 26.8 and Asia Pacific 17.2. Around the world, there are 35 billion online devices (computers, tablets and smartphones) and this number is only going to increase. Nearly every one uses the Internet to chat, send e-mails and play games. In the top ten most used Internet applications, e-mail is at number one (96 per cent of Internet users send e-mails). On an average day we globally send more than 100.000.000 e-mails! According to researchers at the University of Twente, the Internet has undergone a social revolution: research has shown that academics and others with a higher vocational or university degree use the Internet for a greater variety of tasks. However, ordinary people, with a lower educational degree, tend to be the greatest consumers of online media.

The New World of Work

E-coaching is perfectly suited to the New World of Work (a.k.a New Way of Work). According to research group Kluwer, the flexibility to organize your own work and workplace is extremely popular. Employers are also increasingly enthusiastic about embracing the New World of Work. In fact, in the USA, the number of mobile workers is expected to grow to 119.7 million by 2015 and similar growth trends are expected across the globe; In the Asia-Pacific region mobile workers are expected to hit 734.5 million, compared to 546.4 million in 2008 while Western Europe's mobile worker growth should reach 129.5 million by the same date. Countries like Switzerland, the USA, Japan, Great Britain and Germany are knowledge-based economies where 70 per cent of jobs are in the service sector. According to a study conducted by Erasmus@Work, knowledge workers greatly appreciate the New World of Work. And the New World of Work has ushered in a new world of coaching. E-coaching enables personal guidance that is both time and location independent. Remote personal guidance is becoming more and more important to enable organizations and/or managers to maintain contact with their teleworkers and provide the right supervision. In this respect, coaching and e-coaching skills play a crucial role. For the teleworkers themselves, the use of social media is increasingly important in order to keep in contact with both their working environment and their friends.

Expansion of service

Another reason to get started with e-coaching is to expand your current range of services. There are countless ways in which you can use e-coaching to facilitate F2F sessions. In organizations whose main activity is the development of skills and competencies, aftercare in the form of e-coaching can help to convert the newly acquired knowledge into tangible and lasting behavioural change. E-coaching is a highly effective extra service in the personal guidance of clients, and it can also be used for new target groups such as young people or expats who live and work abroad.

1.5 Summary

This chapter introduced you to the world of e-coaching. We first looked at the degree of overlap between e-coaching and the disciplines of e-learning and e-therapy. In general, e-therapy is conducted by means of supply-driven programmes whose structure is modular and protocol-based. The client completes a number of standard modules, conducting sporadic online contact with a professional. Coaching is rarely supply-driven, protocols are infrequently used and personal contact is of essential importance to the nature and structure of the process. In the definition of e-coaching we touched upon the fact that e-coaching can be time and location independent, with the learning and reflection process carried out via both analogue and digital means. We also gave a number of reasons that explain the growing popularity of e-coaching. First, it is because today's society is undergoing a boom in online technology, resulting in a rapidly growing need to work online. Second, it is due to the advent of the New World of Work, which has resulted in a great demand for the flexibility to determine your own work and workplace. A flexible form of coaching is therefore perfectly suited to this new professional environment. E-coaching also perfectly complements and/or extends existing services, such as aftercare for training and education. Now we have discussed the precursors to e-coaching and established a definition of e-coaching, we can use the next chapter to go into greater detail about the different types of e-coaching. E-coaching uses a wide variety of communication media, such as the digital telephone, chat programs or e-mail, each of which has its own characteristics, advantages and disadvantages.

Note

1 Psychoeducation involves providing the client with information about psychological processes, symptoms and syndromes, giving them insight and skills to help them deal with their situation.

2

DIFFERENT TYPES OF E-COACHING

In Chapter 1, we introduced the following definition of e-coaching:

E-coaching is a non-hierarchical developmental partnership between two parties separated by a geographical distance, in which the learning and reflection process is conducted via both analogue and virtual means.

An important part of this definition is that e-coaching is not a new technique or method: it is a new type of coaching. What is different is that the communication is conducted electronically, and can take place via a range of different media. E-coaching can be divided into different categories depending on the communication form used. In this chapter, we describe each of the various types of e-coaching and give a brief summary of the advantages and disadvantages of each type.

2.1 Four types of e-coaching

Within the field of e-coaching, a wide variety of communication channels and tools are available. Communication channels relate to the senses involved, such as seeing, hearing or feeling (spoken word, non-verbal etc. – see Section 3.2.2). Communication tools are the things that make communication possible (see Chapter 3). The nature of the communication is largely determined by the selected medium, and hence the medium defines the type of e-coaching:

1 Coaching via a video link (video coaching).
2 Coaching by phone (telephone coaching).
3 Coaching via a chat program (chat coaching).
4 Coaching via e-mail (e-mail coaching).

Furthermore, the selected medium also affects other aspects that distinguish e-coaching from face-to-face (F2F) coaching. These aspects are:

5   Visibility: Can the coach and client see each other?
6   Proximity: Are the coach and client near each other?
7   Time: Is the communication conducted instantly?
8   Means of expression: How is the communication conducted?

The visibility aspect relates to the physical observability of the communication partners. The presence of the client (and the coach) will always manifest itself in a particular way, although this doesn't necessarily have to be visual: it can also be via the spoken or written word. The four characteristics give each type of e-coaching its own specific manifestation, processes and dynamics. For example, studies show that after an F2F session, e-mail is by far the best medium for conducting a deep, transformational conversation, and that both e-mail coaching and telephone coaching offer the greatest flexibility and opportunities for ad-hoc changes.

In Table 2.1, we have displayed all four types of e-coaching and summarized the associated characteristics. We have also included the characteristics of F2F coaching. This overview clearly shows that video coaching only differs from F2F coaching with respect to one characteristic (proximity), while e-mail coaching differs from F2F in all four aspects. In the following sections we will examine the various types of e-coaching in detail. As telephone coaching is the most widely used type and also functions as a basic component of video coaching, we will discuss this medium first. We will then discuss video and chat coaching. Finally we will examine e-mail coaching. All of the following chapters will relate to the types of coaching in which the written word serves as the primary means of expression, i.e. chat and e-mail coaching.

2.2 Telephone coaching

2.2.1 Characteristics

The most familiar type of e-coaching is telephone coaching. For many years, this type has been used for pragmatic reasons: it saves travelling time and costs. In

TABLE 2.1 Types of e-coaching in comparison with F2F coaching

Type	Proximity	Visibility	Means of expression	Time
F2F coaching	close	yes	spoken	synchronous
Video coaching	remote	yes	spoken	synchronous
Telephone coaching	remote	no	spoken	synchronous
Chat coaching	remote	no	written	synchronous
E-mail coaching	remote	no	written	asynchronous

countries with potentially huge distances between coach and client (e.g. America, Australia, Germany) this type of e-coaching is widely used. It is also a logical and realistic choice for international organizations who wish to coach expats or young overseas talent. This type of e-coaching is still reasonably similar to F2F coaching, as the communication is spoken and synchronous. Its main characteristics are as follows:

- *Visibility* – none: In contrast to F2F, the coach and client cannot see each other. As a result, eye contact is not possible and the coach is also less able to pick up on non-verbal signals in order to steer the coaching session in the right direction.
- *Proximity* – remote: The coach and client are in different geographical locations. This type of coaching is therefore location independent, i.e. it doesn't matter where the coach and client are at the point of contact (as long as they have access to a phone).
- *Time* – synchronous: Just like F2F coaching, the communication takes place in real time, with both coach and client participating in the dialogue. A possible point of concern regarding this aspect is any potential time difference if the coach and client are in different time zones.
- *Means of expression* – spoken: Just as in an F2F session, a verbal conversation takes place.

2.2.2 Modern varieties of telephone coaching

Many developments occurred in the telecom sector since the birth of telephone coaching. As a result, a wide variety of telecommunication applications are now available. These include land lines (via analogue technology), mobile phonemobile phones and Internet calls (via digital technology such as VoIP). Highly advanced mobile phones (smartphones) such as the iPhone, Galaxy, Google Nexus and Blackberry are examples of the huge technological advances in the telecom sector. Using smartphones, telephone coaching can be easily extended and/or comple-mented with special programs (apps) that enable video and/or chat coaching. Examples of such apps include WhatsApp, MSN and Ping.

2.2.3 Disadvantages

The most notable disadvantages are the lack of eye contact and body language. This makes non-verbal communication practically impossible, which is seen as an essential factor in establishing the coach–client relationship. However, some forms of non-verbal communication are available, such as intonation. The volume of the client's voice, the use of pauses and the choice of words also provide a great deal of information about what the client is thinking. Studies show that it is certainly possible to make reasonable assessments of a client based on voice alone. Another disadvantage is latency (delay), which occurs when the transmission from coach to client has to cover a great distance. This can result in the parties talking over each other.

2.2.4 Advantages

There are many advantages of telephone coaching. The lack of travelling saves both time and money. Due to the use of mobile phones, it has also become a literally mobile form of coaching. Studies show that it is certainly possible to make reasonable assessments of a client based on voice alone, because the coach is more able to pick up on tone of voice and pauses when on the phone as there is less distraction from visual senses. Within e-coaching programmes, the telephone can be easily used if the client needs a sparring partner at short notice or requires support (e.g. a pep talk to boost self-confidence). In the following text box, the various advantages of telephone coaching are explained in greater detail.

Spotlight: Telephone lifestyle coaching for kicking bad habits

The male members of a Rotary Club took part in an intervention programme aimed at reducing their Body Mass Index (BMI) and improving healthy-living habits. The programme lasted for four months, with one telephone coaching session per month. During these conversations, habits regarding health, physical exercise and nutrition were discussed. Objectives were also set, with the clients' progress being discussed during the telephone sessions. Every participant agreed a coaching agreement during each session in order to promote self-management. The participants were sent a copy of the agreement in order to remind them of their objectives for the next coaching session.

Upon conclusion of the intervention programme, it was clear that lifestyle coaching by phone had resulted in an improvement in the participants' nutrition, quality of life, well-being and levels of physical exercise. The majority of participants said they would recommend the coaching programme to others.

Extremely satisfied customers

Upon completion of the programme, the vast majority of the clients (90 per cent) stated that the telephone is an excellent and practical means of communication within the coaching programme. Ninety three per cent said that the coach was very flexible regarding scheduling of the sessions. Furthermore, the overwhelming majority were extremely satisfied with the relationship between them and their coach. Clients also had many positive words about many of the coach's qualities, such as listening without judgment, answering questions, giving advice and helping identify obstacles in the path to weight loss. Only 3 per cent of the participants said that they would have preferred face-to-face meetings with the coach.

2.3 Video coaching

2.3.1 Characteristics

Video coaching is conducted via a camera connected to an online PC (known as a webcam). This type of coaching is rapidly growing in popularity. This is due to the fact that nearly all modern-day computers and laptops are equipped with a built-in webcam (including microphone and speakers) as standard. Video coaching is a technologically advanced form of telephone coaching, featuring a video link in addition to a telephone link. Most computers have access to programs that enable video coaching. Just like telephone coaching, this type of e-coaching is mainly used to save on travelling time and costs. Essentially, video coaching is the same as telephone coaching, except it also provides visual images. As a result, this type of e-coaching is the most similar to F2F coaching, as it is only the aspect of proximity that separates the two. The following is a summary of the characteristics of video coaching:

- *Visibility* – via webcam: The coach and client can see each other via a video link. True eye contact is therefore not really possible and the coach is less able to pick-up on non-verbal signals that are normally used to steer coaching sessions in the right direction.
- *Proximity* – remote: This type of e-coaching is also location independent because it doesn't matter where the coach and client are at the moment of contact (as long as they have access to the Internet and the necessary equipment for video communication).
- *Time* – synchronous: The communication takes place in real time as both parties participate in the dialogue at the same time. As with telephone coaching, you must take into account possible time differences if the coach and client are in different time zones.
- *Means of expression* – spoken: Just as in an F2F session, a verbal conversation takes place.

2.3.2 Video coaching via Skype

There are several programs that enable video coaching as Google Hangout ',' Microsoft Lync and 'Skype'. Skype is one of the best-known programs around. It started life as a telecom program that enabled people to make free phone calls over the Internet to other Skype users. Since then, Skype has added a video function, which makes video coaching possible. Many other functionalities have also been added, such as chat, file sharing and screenshot sharing between users. For example, if a coach wants to explain how a website works, then he/she can send a screenshot to the client, enabling them to view the website together. Conference calls with multiple parties are also possible via Skype. As Skype's software is extremely user-friendly and free to use for practically all users and computers, it is very frequently used as a vehicle for video coaching. As a result, video coaching is often referred to as *Skype coaching*.

2.3.3 Mobile video coaching

Due to lightning-fast technological development within the telecoms and computer sectors, video coaching is becoming extremely popular. More and more mobile phones and tablets (portable computers such as the iPad) are equipped with cameras as standard, enabling video calls. However, in practice, an excellent quality Internet connection is required in order to constantly maintain the video link. If a strong connection is not available, then interference, delays and noise are likely to disrupt the conversation. For this reason, coaches often decide to use the camera at the beginning of the call and then turn it off later. This ensures that the conversation starts off on a more personal note. This is therefore effectively a switch from video coaching to telephone coaching.

2.3.4 Disadvantages

The main disadvantage of video coaching is the fact that a fast and stable Internet connection is required to maintain a good quality video link. However, thanks to modern technology such as fibre-optic cables and sophisticated devices, this is becoming less and less of a problem. A second disadvantage relates to the visibility aspect: because the client is technically visible to the coach, it would seem that there is little difference between video coaching and a face-to-face session. However, the video link doesn't give a full picture. In general, only the upper torso and face are visible, with hand and arm movements mostly occurring out of the camera's view. Furthermore, the video link gives the illusion of eye contact, although in reality this is not the case. This is because the face displayed on-screen is at eye-level, while the webcam is usually at the top of the computer and therefore roughly level with the top of the person's head. As a result, it is virtually impossible to look each other directly in the eyes. The limited availability of body language and the lack of eye contact results in a lesser degree of non-verbal communication. Another possible disadvantage relating to visibility is that there can be elements that distract attention from the dialogue, such as an eye-catching painting or background. Any such elements within either camera's field of vision should be removed or covered-up.

It is therefore important that the coach is aware of the above restrictions and doesn't simply see video coaching as a remote form of F2F coaching, but knows how video-coaching can be favourable to an online coaching programme.

2.3.5 Advantages

Video coaching shares the same advantages as telephone coaching. You save time and money by eliminating the need to travel, and sophisticated portable devices have made it a literally mobile form of coaching. It is also easy to schedule and reschedule sessions (depending on the availability and contactability of the coach), which provides a large degree of flexibility within the coaching process. Skype coaching is extremely handy if the client needs a sparring partner or support at short notice (e.g. a pep talk to boost self-confidence). Recorded video-coaching sessions could be beneficial to coaches for supervision or logging for accreditation purposes.

2.4 Chat coaching

2.4.1 Characteristics

Chat coaching is coaching via a chat program. Chat programs enable you to conduct written conversations between two or more connected computers. Via their keyboards, the coach and client type text into the chat program on their computers, with the typed text appearing practically instantaneously on the other person's screen once it is sent. As with telephone coaching, this type of e-coaching is mainly used to eliminate travelling time/costs. Chat coaching differs from both telephone and video coaching with regard to one important aspect: the communication is written rather than spoken. The main characteristics of chat coaching are as follows:

- *Visibility* – none: The coach and client cannot see or hear each other. As a result, nearly all non-verbal communication is omitted.
- *Proximity* – remote: This type of e-coaching is also location independent because it doesn't matter where the coach and client are at the moment of contact (as long as they have access to the Internet and all equipment required for chat communication).
- *Time* – synchronous: The communication takes place more or less in real time as both parties participate in the dialogue at the same time. However, it is less fluent than a regular conversation, as there is waiting time involved between sending a message and receiving a response. Also, you must take into account possible time differences if the coach and client are in different time zones.
- *Means of expression* – written: Communication is entirely text-based, with various linguistic tools used by the coach in order to ensure the dialogue runs smoothly and effectively.

2.4.2 Linguistic tools

Chat conversations take longer than face-to-face conversations. The reason for this is that typing takes longer than speaking, and you therefore have to wait relatively longer for a response. Both parties must be patient and wait until the other sends a reply. You can use a variety of linguistic tools to facilitate this process and minimize waiting time, such as writing messages that are only 1–2 lines long, writing telegram-style messages or abbreviating words/common expressions (e.g. cu2m = see you tomorrow). Another tool that is increasingly used is the emoticon (also known as a 'smiley'). These are symbols that express emotions in chat conversations. A smiley is a symbolic representation of a smiling face :-) By using these techniques, chat conversations can convey both information and emotions via a few brief lines of text. See Chapter 3 for a complete overview of all available linguistic tools.

2.4.3 Two new elements in the coaching process

Within this type of e-coaching, the coach and client do not have to see or hear each other in order to conduct a dialogue. The lack of visibility of the coach and the switch from spoken to written dialogue introduce two new elements within the coaching process. This creates a situation that differs fundamentally from F2F coaching:

1   *Social anonymity:* Within chat coaching, the client's body language, posture and appearance are no longer visible. In other words, less direct information about the client is available. For many coaches, this seems to be an impossible task, as the prevailing philosophy within the coaching profession is that without body language or other non-verbal information, it is impossible to build up a coach–client relationship. However, numerous studies have shown that this is not the case. On the contrary, not being able to see or hear the client can even be beneficial, thanks in part to the feeling of anonymity that is created. As a result, the client feels less pressured with regard to a number of matters, such as socially desirable behaviour, their appearance or a feeling that the coach is judging them. This makes it easier and quicker to get to the heart of the matter. This does require extra effort on the coach's part, as they will have to learn a different way of steering and shaping the dialogue and the coaching programme. See Chapter 4 for more detailed information about social anonymity.

2   *Written communication rather than spoken communication:* Writing is associated with improving insight, self-reflection, optimism, self-esteem and a feeling of being in control. Various studies have shown that writing about particular events helps the brain to cognitively and emotionally process them more effectively. Using an expressive writing style to give meaning and context to emotional events can be particularly helpful in bringing about positive changes in behaviour. By asking the client to chat in this way, brief sessions can greatly facilitate awareness and behavioural change. Furthermore, typing out the text rather than voicing it can save the information either analogue or digital form. By storing the texts, you maintain a physical record of the entire coaching process that can be reviewed as many times as you wish. See Chapter 3 and 4 for further explanation about the effect of the written word within the field of coaching.

2.4.4 Availability of chat coaching

Chat coaching can be facilitated by a variety of chat programs, such as Google Talk, ICQ and Facebook Chat as well as smartphone applications such as WhatsApp, Facebook Messenger, Telegram, Blackberry Messenger, iMessage and Ping. In addition, Skype and other well-known communication programs (such as Yahoo and Gmail), and special websites (such as Chatten.nl, Chat-avenue.com, and Pluform.com) also offer chat programs. See Chapter 10 for more information about the safety and security of these type of applications.

2.4.5 Disadvantages

The main disadvantage of chat coaching is the lack of visibility of the client. Learning to deal with the lack of body language, eye contact and other well-known forms of non-verbal communication is a major challenge for any coach.

Another disadvantage is the short delays in each dialogue due to the time required to type, read and wait for messages. This can cause different subjects to overlap each other and disrupt the flow of the conversation, resulting in unexpected or redundant messages. This 'one-way traffic' can create confusion. In addition, the waiting time involved makes it tempting to try and multitask – one or both parties may become distracted and start to combine activities. This can create the impression that you are not concentrating. A third disadvantage is that the language skills of either the coach or the client could cause problems. It is important that the coach's language is flawless, and the speed of chat communication means that errors are easy to make. It is therefore important that you check your spelling and grammar before sending each message, which requires a great degree of care and attention on the coach's part. The client's language skills are less vital, with errors being much less of a problem. The coach must make sure the client feels comfortable and capable enough to express him/herself.

2.4.6 Advantages

Chat coaching has the same advantages as telephone coaching. Time and money is saved as travelling is unnecessary, and the use of sophisticated portable devices has made this a literally mobile form of coaching. Chat coaching sessions can be easily scheduled and rescheduled depending on the availability and contactability of the coach. This ensures a significant degree of flexibility within coaching programs.

The new aspects introduced by chat coaching – social anonymity and the written word – can both be viewed as advantages. The anonymity means that clients feel less inhibited, and expressing themselves in writing means that clients get to the heart of the matter quicker. Due to these factors, chat coaching is particularly useful at times when the client needs a sparring partner at short notice or when the coaching objective is being clearly defined. Also in the case of chat coaching, saved chat coaching sessions can serve the purpose of supervision or logging for accreditation for the coach.

2.5 E-mail coaching

2.5.1 Characteristics

Electronic mail, or e-mail for short, is a form of digital post. E-mail communication dates back to the 1970s and is the most widely used form of online communication (although usage amongst the younger generation is now declining). In effect, e-mail is the same as chat communication, except more waiting time is involved between responses. As with chat communication, the messages between coach and client are typed into an e-mail program via a computer keyboard before being sent to the recipient. This form of communication is very similar to the classic art of letter writing, which is as old as the written word itself. However, thanks to computers and the Internet, the response time is much shorter in comparison to conventional post. As a result, you could refer to e-mail as 'typed conversations'. This type of text-based coaching we call e-mail coaching. E-mail coaching, just like all other types of e-coaching, is primarily used to cut travelling time and costs. E-mail coaching differs from the other types of e-coaching with regard to one important aspect – asynchronous communication (see Chapters 3 and 4 for a more detailed explanation). The characteristics of e-mail coaching are as follows:

- *Visibility* – none: The coach and client cannot see or hear each other. As a result, nearly all non-verbal communication is impossible.
- *Proximity* – remote: As well as being location independent, e-mail coaching is also time independent because it doesn't matter where the coach and client are or when the moment of contact takes place (as long as they have access to the Internet and the equipment required for e-mail communication).
- *Time* – asynchronous: The communication does not take place simultaneously. Both coach and client decide for themselves when to communicate, and the interaction between them is therefore delayed. Frequently, periods of hours, days or even weeks can elapse between responses.
- *Means of expression* – written: The communication is entirely text-based, sent from screen to screen. Here also, various linguistic tools can be used in order to ensure the dialogue runs smoothly and effectively.

2.5.2 Linguistic tools

E-mail conversations take longer than F2F conversations. This is because typing and reading take longer than speaking and listening. In addition, wrongly interpreted messages can cause miscommunication, which takes more time to explain due to the asynchronous nature of the communication. We therefore advise that for e-mail coaching, you don't use the time-saving measures designed for chat coaching (e.g. limiting message length to 1–2 lines, writing telegram-style messages and abbreviating words/expressions). However, other linguistic tools, such as using emoticons, are acceptable as they can help add context and improve understanding of the messages. Coaches can also use tools to first analyse the client's messages and second select the best response strategy. See Chapter 6 for more explanation of linguistic tools.

2.5.3 Three new elements within the coaching process

E-mail coaching involves a number of elements that do not apply to F2F coaching. In addition to social anonymity and the written word (also associated with chat coaching), e-mail coaching involves a third new aspect – *asynchronicity*.

Asynchronicity is when the coach and client don't have to be simultaneously present whilst conducting the coaching dialogue. This makes the coaching programme much more flexible as both coach and client can send the messages whenever and wherever they choose. Furthermore, the client can decide for him/herself how often and how much they wish to write (qualitative and quantitative), when to take breaks, and whether to edit, correct or delete any or all of what they have written. The autonomy of the client is boosted, giving him/her a much more active role in the coaching process and greater influence over their coaching programme. This in turn creates a feeling of emotional control and comfort. In effect, e-coaching transfers a great deal of control from the coach to the client. By releasing them from the need to travel to particular locations at particular times, it is possible to increase the number of contact moments. This enables the coach to take smaller steps in the process and divide up assignments and behavioural experiments into bite-size chunks. This reduces the difficulty level of the tasks and therefore increases the number of successes experienced by the client. All of this is made possible by the asynchronicity of e-mail communication, which enables the coach to better adapt the coaching process to suit the individual needs of the client. See Chapter 4 for more detailed explanation of the effects of social anonymity, written communication and asynchronicity on the coaching process.

2.5.4 Additional possibilities

Communication via e-mail offers a number of extra opportunities. As well as enabling you to refer to information on the Internet (via hyperlinks), it is also possible to send multimedia data. Linear writing (such as in letters) is increasingly giving way to 'multidirectionality', as sections of text can be easily edited, organized or amended. This flexibility means that the content and structure of the text can be developed throughout the writing process. It is also possible to insert and archive messages. E-mails can be linked to previous e-mails to create a dialogue structure. You can also use 'quote techniques': both parties can copy and paste quantities of text into their messages. They can also add their own comments and opinions to this copied text, using a different colour, font etc. in order to make it clear that this is the person's own view, and not part of the original text.

2.5.5 Using e-mail programs

The production, sending and formatting of e-mails depend on the e-mail programs used by both sender and recipient. As a result, the sender can never be certain of exactly how the sent e-mail will be displayed to the recipient. It is therefore advisable for the coach to use the same e-mail program as the client. E-mail coaching can be facilitated by a variety of e-mail programs (such as Outlook, Mozilla Thunderbird, and Pegasus Mail, Sparrow) or via the Internet (web-based programs such as Outlook.com, Yahoo mail and Gmail). A relatively new type of e-mail coaching is SMS (Short Message System) coaching, which uses very short messages. These messages are very similar to the messages used in chat coaching, except that communication by SMS coaching is asynchronous. SMS coaching is suitable for giving clients a motivational boost and is therefore a useful supplement to other types of e-coaching and F2F coaching. However, we advise coaches to gain experience with chat and e-mail coaching before getting started with SMS coaching.

For a more detailed explanation of the security and privacy issues regarding e-mail programs, see Chapter 10.

2.5.6 Disadvantages

As with chat coaching, the main disadvantage of e-mail coaching is the lack of visibility of the client. The coach's communication with the client is in the form of text, which necessitates the use of tools (such as linguistic analysis) to evaluate the relationship and structure the coaching process. The coach must therefore learn new skills before coaching is possible based on written communication alone.

Another disadvantage is the theoretical possibility for coaching to be available 24/7. E-mails can be sent to the recipient in a matter of seconds, and this speed can create higher expectations. The sender assumes that their e-mail will be answered within a relatively short amount of time. The coach must therefore employ expectation management and ensure that clear agreements and boundaries are established regarding their communication. Finally, the coach must have the necessary language skills to ensure that misinterpretations are kept to a minimum. After all, once an e-mail is sent, it is difficult to recall.

2.5.7 Advantages

The advantages of e-mail coaching match those of the other types of e-coaching. It saves travelling time and costs, and thanks to modern portable devices, it has become a literally mobile form of coaching. E-mails can be composed at any desired moment, dependent only on the availability of the sender. This ensures maximum flexibility within the coaching programme. Also for e-mail coaching counts that saved e-mail coaching conversations can serve the purpose of supervision or logging for accreditation for the coach.

All of the advantages of the extra process elements associated with e-mail coaching (e.g. asynchronicity, social anonymity and written communication) are discussed in detail in the next chapter.

2.6 Summary

This chapter explained how e-coaching is not a completely new coaching discipline, but merely a new method of delivery. This new method can in turn be divided into separate categories depending on the medium used to conduct the communication. The different types of e-coaching are telephone coaching, video coaching, chat coaching and e-mail coaching. These four types of e-coaching differ from face-to-face (F2F) coaching in relation to four key aspects: visibility (can the coach and client see each other?), proximity (are the coach and client in the same place?), time (is the communication synchronous or asynchronous?) and the means of expression (how is the communication conducted?). By examining these four aspects, it is evident that video coaching is the most similar to F2F coaching and that e-mail coaching differs from F2F the most.

We then examined the advantages and disadvantages of every type of e-coaching before introducing a number of extra elements associated with chat and e-mail coaching, i.e. social anonymity (being physically separated from the coach), asynchronicity (lack of simultaneous involvement during the communication process) and the written word (as opposed to spoken communication). By switching from spoken to written communication and using the Internet, a new communication method has entered the coaching profession: written e-communication. This new means of communication has had a significant effect on the coach–client relationship and the coaching process. Therefore, in the next chapter, we will put this method of communication under the microscope, examining a number of interesting theories about written e-communication and why, when used correctly, it can be so effective at accommodating clients' individual needs and wishes.

3

E-COMMUNICATION

The new world of communication

In Chapter 2, we explained that there are many types of e-coaching and that they can be categorized according to the communication medium used. The medium often requires the communication to be conducted differently from traditional F2F coaching. This is particularly the case for chat and e-mail coaching, as the communication is conducted entirely in writing and does not involve verbal communication. Written communication is as old as the written word itself, although communication via Internet messaging has its own set of rules and dynamics. Within this type of online communication, the processes are conducted using different devices and via various channels, such as digital telecoms, e-mail, chat programs and text messages. Within the field of linguistics, many studies have been conducted into this type of 'computer mediated communication'. Most types of e-coaching are simply forms of regular coaching that make use of written e-communication. In this chapter, we will explain this type of communication in greater detail.

3.1 Characteristics of e-communication

The umbrella term for various types of e-communication is 'computer mediated communication' (CMC). One of the main characteristics of CMC is that people can connect without both people being physically present. It has been shown that physical presence during communication (proximity) is not a decisive factor in establishing a feeling of intimacy or intensity during communication. It is a fallacy that body language and eye contact are essential in order to develop a good coach–client relationship. To illustrate this, recent research into online therapy showed that 86 per cent of clients receiving therapy exclusively by e-mail reported that they found it to be a very positive and personable form of therapy. Other recent research in the field of online therapy showed that clients scored initiative, trust, and spontaneity higher in non-face-to-face conditions. This is a great eye-opener for many coaches who have always been taught that 70–90 per cent of communication consists of non-verbal signals. For more information about this fallacy, see the text box 'Spotlight: Myth busting regarding non-verbal communication'. When referring to e-communication we mean written type of e-communication.

CMC can be divided into two categories: synchronous and asynchronous communication. With synchronous (simultaneous) communication, both parties are actively communicating at the same time, as is the case for telephone, video and chat coaching. One precondition for synchronous written communication is that the messages are received with little to no delay, i.e. the message is almost instantly visible on the recipient's screen, eliciting an immediate response. The second type of CMC is asynchronous (non-simultaneous) communication. The term asynchronous therefore indicates that the communication takes place at different moments in time.

Spotlight: Myth busting regarding non-verbal communication

There are a number of widely held assumptions regarding non-verbal communication. The most frequently quoted proportion is that 7 per cent of communication is verbal and 93 per cent is non-verbal. The source quoted for this statistic is the work of psychologist Albert Mehrabian. The results of two studies he carried out in 1967 show that 7 per cent of communication is conducted verbally, 38 per cent is based on intonation and 55 per cent is communicated via body language. However, his studies only related to expressing your own emotions, i.e. if you want to show that you are happy, then say that you are happy, say it in a happy voice and adopt friendly and open body language. These studies therefore relate to consciously communicating your own emotions. Nowadays, we know that a large proportion of our communication is subconscious and involves more than simply expressing our own emotions. Since Mehrabian's work, hundreds of new studies have shown that the words we choose are also important and that non-verbal aspects play a much smaller role in our communication than previously thought. Even today, Mehrabian himself continues to oppose the widespread misinterpretation of his research results.

3.2 Omission of communication

E-communication eliminates a large degree of non-verbal communication. This is generally seen as a disadvantage. The typical mind set of coaches learning e-coaching for the first time is 'it's too impersonal, too much vital information is lost and it is too difficult to compensate for this lost information'. In traditional F2F situations, the physical presence of the coach plays a role in the associated social and non-verbal signals. For e-mail and chat coaching, the client is not physically present and communication is exclusively written. Visual and auditory information is lost, and therefore many clues that can help you quickly assess the situation are not available. When human beings lived in nomadic groups on the savannahs, it became imperative for survival that we learned to quickly read the body language of our tribal brethren to detect potential threats, even if the person had their backs to us. There are a number of theories within CMC regarding the loss of this information. This information is predominantly social, such as elements of people's appearance to which stereotypes are attached (how we dress, hairstyles, tattoos, jewellery etc.) This provides information about a person and is interpreted by other people in accordance with their own individual values and beliefs. In the following sections, we will examine the channel reduction model and filter model.

3.2.1 Channel reduction theory

Channel reduction theory is a term that has become well-known since the introduction of the channel reduction model. This model shows that when the number of communication channels is reduced, information is lost. One example of a lost communication channel within CMC is non-verbal communication, such as facial expressions, intonation and hand/arm gestures. Here, channel reduction takes place as the person you are communicating with is not present, the communication is conducted exclusively in writing and all other communication channels present in F2F coaching have been eliminated. The loss of these communication channels therefore reduces the observational ability of your counterpart. In other words, you have fewer opportunities to express yourself, and hence vital information could be lost. Other examples of lost non-verbal communication are the lack of eye contact and the inability to hear subtle changes of intonation, which makes it more difficult to immediately detect and correct any misunderstandings that may occur. It has also been shown that channel reduction can result in clients asking less spontaneous questions.

3.2.2 Filter model

Another model that describes the omission of information is the filter model. This model concentrates on how the use of CMC 'filters out' important information from the message. In the case of e-mail and chat, visual physical information is filtered out, such as any information that communicates the status or power of either party. Examples of this include static indicators such as clothes or hairstyle, and dynamic indicators such as facial expressions and/or gestures. Auditory information that is filtered out includes interjections such as 'hmm' or 'oh, yes', which subtly show the person is listening, agreeing etc. The aspects that are communicated to each party therefore change considerably. The visual and auditory information is important as it helps you to create a mental picture of your conversation partner, which in turn allows you to assess their reliability or credibility. These processes are based on learned associations (e.g. a man in his fifties with grey hair would be associated with life experience and wisdom).

3.3 Using linguistic tools

In the previous sections, we have described how non-verbal information is omitted by using e-communication, especially the visual and auditory information that is not conveyed by writing alone. However, not all non-verbal information is omitted. This is because language in e-communication can be enriched using linguistic tools. These tools, such as emoticons and sound/action words, can be used to express our emotions or current state of mind. The following is a description of the various linguistic tools available:

- *Emoticons* are used as a vehicle for expressing emotions. These symbols visually simulate the omitted physical aspects of communication. Various studies show that emoticons are very effective at reflecting the facial expressions, frame of mind and tone of the conversation, which enriches the communication. Although different emoticons perform different functions, they all help to express the identity of the sender and help you to correctly interpret the text. The smiley is the most famous example of an emoticon. It is written as :) or :-) and is often incorrectly interpreted by computers as the upper case letter J. It is usually placed at the end of a sentence. :)
- *Sound words* such as 'hmm' or 'ugh' imitate auditory expressions or indicate spontaneous thoughts. The intensity of the words can be varied by doubling letters or repeating the words.
- *Action words* help describe reactions to situations by placing the indicative form of a verb between asterisks (e.g. ★smiles★, ★gulps★, ★hopes that this is a good enough example★).
- *Emphasis fonts* such as **boldface**, *italics* or different colours conspicuously mark or accentuate words, or sentences, helping to draw attention to them.
- *Alternative writing styles* can be employed to exaggerate certain points, such as alternative/exaggerated spelling (such as 'oooooooooh'), repeated punctuation marks (I can't wait for you to get here!!!!!!!!!!!!!), using smaller or larger font sizes, adding s p a c e s b e t w e e n l e t t e r s or using CAPITAL LETTERS (although this usually indicates that you are shouting and can therefore come across as rude).

By using the above symbols and tools, you can help to make a text-based conversation more authentic. Ultimately, the decision of whether to use them and which to use depends on contextual and relationship-related aspects such as the mutual trust (how well do I know this person?), who the person is (young/old, male/female etc.), or the subject matter (positive, personal, distressing etc.).

Although different emoticons perform different functions, they all help to express the identity of the sender and help you to correctly interpret the written text. Besides the main differences in the meaning of these emoticons, they are used differently across cultures. The ever popular smiley will be written as ^_^ in the East. The smiley in Western countries will be written as :-). According to a research by Yuki, Maddux and Masuda this difference in writing style is due to the norms of expressing emotions in Eastern and Western countries. Since openly expressing emotions is not common in the East, people tend to focus more on the eyes in interpreting emotions, whereas in the West people are used to openly expressing emotions and will focus on cues in the mouth. Additional to writing style differences, the aim of using emoticons depends on cultural norms as well. One study tested these differences amongst American, Turkish and Korean participants. Both American and Turkish respondents used emoticons in order to express their emotions and to avoid misunderstanding. Koreans on the other hand, would use these emoticons to express their gratefulness. Despite these cross-cultural differences, emoticons are used in different cultures.

3.4 Enriched communication

Section 3.2 shows how communication by phone, chat or e-mail can cause problems due to the lack of non-verbal communication. In Section 3.3, we described a number of linguistic tools that can partially compensate for the lack of non-verbal communication. However, recent insights into e-communication have shown that the lack of non-verbal communication can actually benefit the dialogue in a number of ways.

For example, the lack of visual social information about your conversation partner can help remove social inhibitions, obstacles and feelings of privilege or control. One result of channel reduction is that it removes constraints and promotes participation, equality, friendliness, openness and honesty (a more detailed explanation of this effect is given in Chapter 4). The relaxation of inhibitions can also spiral into antisocial behaviour such as rudeness, hostility or overstepping boundaries, although this rarely happens as the central focus of e-coaching is to nurture a development partnership based on equality and mutual respect. In the following subsections, we will discuss two theories that explain how a rich dialogue can be achieved despite the lack of non-verbal communication.

3.4.1 The filter-in model

Recent research shows that problems on a social or relationship level are by no means inevitable within e-communication and that the emotional aspect is not necessarily reduced. The visual and auditory information that is filtered out can be expressed in a completely different way, which compensates for the omission of traditional forms of non-verbal communication. The online conversation partners develop new social skills that replace and complement the lost information and enable satisfactory communication. This is known as the 'filter-in' model. The online conversation partners replace the lost social information and are more meticulous when reading the existing social information. By only communicating in writing, you are more capable of deciding which information to disclose and to whom you disclose it. It enables you to deviate from your real-life identity without the other person noticing. This visual anonymity helps people to optimize the way they digitally present themselves and removes any worries they may have about their appearance, which results in happier and more relaxed communication. Some researchers even take things further, and have shown that CMC interaction enables friendlier, more sociable and more intimate communication than F2F interaction. The quicker exchange of more intimate information benefits the experience and the effectiveness of the communication, which helps to deepen the relationship and bring the parties together. This is known as 'hyper personal communication'.

3.4.2 CMC is 'hyper personal'

The *hyper personal model* is an interpersonal communication theory that suggests CMC can enable even closer personal connection as it goes beyond the boundaries of F2F interaction. CMC offers users a wide range of benefits. Clients are given strategic control regarding what information they wish to disclose and how they wish to present it. The Hyper personal communication in CMC is more socially desirable communication than we tend to experience in parallel F2F situations. This perspective also suggests that CMC users experience a greater degree of intimacy and sympathy within the coach–client relationship than similar relationships based on F2F interaction. The CMC user is part of the hyper personal communication, meaning that both sender and recipient are involved in the process of selective self-presentation via the messages they formulate and choose to send. The communication partners are much more in control of how they present themselves to the other person by optimizing their self-presentation. This can result in both communication partners idealizing the other because of crediting qualities and meaning to the other based on the available non–verbal signals (conveyed by linguistic tools) found in the text, and which give a personal feel to the message. This process is reinforced by the asynchronous nature of the communication, as both sender and recipient have plenty of time to read and consider the messages they send and receive. The task of writing the messages can also be split up into more bite-size chunks. Messages can be saved at any point, allowing you to come back later to either finish it off, rewrite it or edit at a convenient moment. The communication can be organized and scheduled in accordance with the other person's wishes and needs. In this way, hyper personal communication can go beyond the boundaries of traditional interpersonal communication. In other words, online relationships can become much more personal than F2F relationships.

Optimistic expectations and the prospect of a long-term relationship help to create a positive synergy between coach and client. When meeting someone for the first time, we start with a positive outlook about the person. This is because for our own self-image, we like to believe our conversation partner is someone special.

After all, getting attention from someone special helps confirm your value as a person. Clients frequently attribute a wide range of positive attributes to the coach, and these ideals usually remain intact as long as the coach doesn't do anything that shatters the illusion.

In the case of e-mail coaching, every friendly e-mail from the coach serves as a confirmation of the positive image in the client's mind, and helps to reinforce their affinity for the coach. E-mail coaching involves a high frequency of contact within the coaching process (see also Section 4.1, item 2). This reinforces the relationship and facilitates the mutual exchange of positive thoughts and feelings, which benefits the quality of the coaching process. Exchanging positive thoughts and feelings (compliments) is also an important element in F2F coaching. However, it is important to note that expressing or receiving compliments and positive thoughts/feelings can make some people feel uncomfortable. In Chapter 8, we address this phenomenon in greater detail. In addition to sending positive messages, there are many other ways to help the communication run as smoothly as possible. For example, e-mails that contain both verbal politeness indicators (e.g. 'please' and 'thanks') and structural politeness indicators (e.g. starting letters with 'Dear ....' and closing with 'Yours sincerely') are more likely to elicit a polite response. The strategic control of interpersonal communication within CMC can therefore facilitate and strengthen the relationship between coach and client.

3.5 Summary

In this chapter, we investigated how e-coaching limits communication opportunities by preventing traditional non-verbal communication. Video coaching retains a limited degree of non-verbal communication, while e-mail coaching eliminates it almost entirely, replacing it with new types of non-verbal communication. On the one hand, the increased likelihood of misinterpretation, assumptions and wrongly drawn conclusions can make written e-communication difficult, while on the other hand, computer mediated communication (CMC) offers new opportunities for building an effective and amicable relationship with the client. CMC also offers the possibility of 'hyper personal' communication, as the senders are able to devote as much time and attention as they wish in order to fine-tune the messages and selectively present themselves to the recipient. They can also read and review the messages in their own time. In addition to this, linguistic tools can be used that express the sender's emotions and state of mind, such as emoticons (e.g. smilies or other symbols), sound words, action words, emphasis fonts and alternative spellings/writing styles. We also learned that if a coach wants to harness the benefits of written e-communication, then it is important that they acquire and continually develop the competencies required for effective e-coaching. For this purpose, Chapters 5 and 6 give extensively explanation of how coaches can get the most out of written e-communication and optimally facilitate their coaching practice. However, before we get to this, we will explain the fifteen essential ingredients of optimal e-coaching in Chapter 4.

4

THE POWER OF E-COACHING

Most coaches already make use of e-communication in their coaching practice, particularly e-mails and phone calls. Given the demographics in the modern, globalized world we live in, this is a logical step. In large countries such as the USA, Brazil, Canada, Australia, Germany and the UK, e-coaching is primarily used in order to eliminate the time and expense that travelling involves. This is the most frequently given reason for using e-coaching. However, as we have already seen in Chapters 2 and 3, e-communication also offers a wide variety of other benefits depending on the communication medium used. In this chapter, we will list all of these learning and development benefits and explain the many active ingredients that accelerate and reinforce the e-coaching process. First, we will summarize these fifteen aspects, and then we will explain the three underlying process elements. These descriptions are based on an extensive literature study and the practical experiences of over 150 coaches and clients. Some of these aspects can also be applied in F2F coaching. However, for many of these aspects, the costs involved would make them impractical for F2F.

4.1 The fifteen ingredients of e-coaching

The fifteen ingredients do not apply equally to all types of e-coaching. The more each type differs from F2F coaching, the more applicable these fifteen aspects will be (see also Section 2.1: Four types of e-coaching).

1. Location and time independence
E-coaching via video, telephone, chat and e-mail is location independent. The coach and client are not in the same room and no travelling time is required to allow the coaching to take place. Normally, the coach and/or client would have to spend a significant part of the working day travelling to a 1 or 2-hour coaching

session. With e-coaching, no travelling is necessary. E-mail coaching goes one step further, offering time independence (asynchronicity) in addition to location independence. This enables maximum time efficiency as the clients themselves are able to decide when to contact the coach. Messages can be written and sent by e-mail whenever and wherever the client chooses, whether they are at work in the morning, on the train in the afternoon or at the gym in the evening. They can also send messages after particular incidents, at times of doubt or during a period of reflection. All types of e-coaching eliminate the cost of travelling, parking and accommodation that are associated with traditional F2F coaching. Finally, it is highly advantageous that both coach and client can decide for themselves from where they wish to contact each other. All of these advantages greatly increase the flexibility within the coaching programme, enabling both parties to optimally fit the coaching into their schedule.

2. Frequent contact

By communicating online or by phone during the coaching process, it is possible to structure the program to include frequent coaching contact. In general, a coaching programme consists of a series of planned sessions with relatively long gaps between them (e.g. two or three weeks apart, sometimes as many as four). Research has shown that the frequency of contact between coach and client is significantly proportional to the success of the coaching programme. The more interpersonal contact, the more successful the client considers the coaching to be. E-coaching makes it physically and financially viable to greatly increase the frequency of contact and greatly reduce the time between contact moments. You can also arrange a series of online sessions to accelerate the process. In this scenario, the coach and client are in contact twice or three times per week. Some coaches even offer concentrated coaching programmes, in which very frequent contact is conducted over the course of a single week. For such programmes, it is important that the client has enough time for the numerous sessions involved. Within e-coaching, the contact moments can be flexibly scheduled, ensuring continuity within the coaching process and facilitating lively interaction with plenty of opportunities for feedback. It also gives the client greater control of the tempo and intensity of the coaching, so the process can be accelerated or decelerated in accordance with the client's needs and the amount of time and/or energy they are able to devote to the coaching.

3. Baby steps

A frequent pitfall in the process of behavioural change is trying to do too much too soon. Biting off more than you can chew drastically reduces the chances of success, which in turn robs the client of the motivation they need to persevere. Coaching programmes that fail to take this into consideration are frequently unsuccessful. However, with e-coaching, you can schedule frequent contact moments, which enables you to take smaller steps. As a result, assignments, exercises and behavioural experiments can be broken up into bite-size chunks, which decrease the difficulty level and therefore minimize the chance of failure. The client therefore experiences more moments of success, which is a key aspect in any learning process. The greater number of successes boosts the client's motivation and limits the impact of any setbacks. Clients can share their moments of triumph with the coach very quickly (or straight away in the case of e-mail coaching), instead of having to wait days or weeks until the next F2F session as is the case with F2F coaching. The coach can then positively reinforce the achievement and motivate the client to take the next step. In the event of setbacks, the coach can reassure the client and encourage them to take a smaller step. This helps prevent the coaching process from stagnating in the event that something goes wrong.

4. On-the-job learning

The definition of e-coaching in Chapter 1 states that e-coaching is carried out in real-life situations that are relevant to the client. In addition to digital tasks such as online learning and reflection, the client must also carry out analogue tasks. By analogue tasks, we mean activities (such as exercises, assignments and behavioural experiments) within the client's everyday surroundings, such as at work or at home. As the client carries out these tasks in familiar surroundings, the relevance of the coaching is maximized. This is because the client will literally experience how certain actions result in particular reactions from their environment. With the assistance of the coach, the client can then reflect upon these actions. This principle facilitates what is known as *transfer of coaching*, or in other words, the application of the client's new knowledge and skills in their everyday life.

5. High level of engagement

Within coaching programmes, the client's level of engagement increases as the next session nears. The peak level is achieved during the session, after which it decreases steadily as time goes by. This cycle is repeated several times during F2F coaching programmes. However, with e-coaching, this cycle can be broken. Due to the frequent contact moments, the smaller steps and the greater relevance of the learning environment, the client can be 'sucked into' the process, greatly increasing the intensity with which the client works on the programme. The frequent contact and the continual virtual presence of the coach promotes greater engagement between the two parties, which is a decisive factor in how the client experiences the coaching relationship. In turn, a good coaching relationship is one of the most important factors in the success of a coaching programme. Figure. 4.1 displays the client's level of engagement within both regular coaching and e-coaching programmes.

6. Straight to the point

Studies show that the first session of an F2F coaching programme is more emotionally draining than the first session of an online programme. This is because with F2F sessions, a relatively large amount of time and energy is spent creating a safe environment for the client. This is necessary in order to ensure a functional

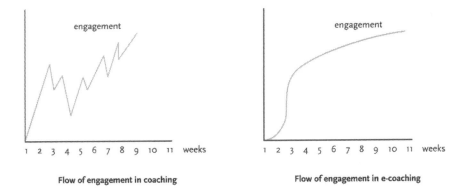

FIGURE 4.1 The client's level of engagement in coaching and e-coaching programs

working relationship and ensure a 'click' between coach and client. With e-coaching, the coach and client do not need to be in the same place in order to conduct the dialogue. They can therefore pick a location in familiar surroundings, e.g. at home or at the workplace. Being in familiar surroundings helps make the client feel safe and in control of the process. Chat and e-mail coaching amplifies this effect even further due to the fact that the coach and client can't see each other (the anonymity principle). As a result, the client tends to open up more to the coach and speak more freely. Within e-coaching, distractions such as *small talk* and socially desirable behaviour are eliminated, while in F2F coaching, they are necessary in order to establish a productive relationship. Consequently, e-coaching gets to the heart of the matter quicker and enables greater depth than F2F coaching.

7. Optimal focus
Coaches and clients who make use of online communication (especially telephone or video coaching) often report that they have to contend with more environmental distractions (such as background noise) than with F2F coaching. As a result, both parties have to maintain greater levels of concentration during the dialogue. Although concentrating so intensely requires much more energy, it also ensures that every one remains optimally focused. With e-mail and chat coaching there is more opportunity for reflection. This is because both coach and client have much more time to think longer and harder, write down their thoughts, review them and add to them if desired. These are intensive cognitive processes that require peace, quiet and concentration. The increased concentration levels result in a more intensive focus on the activity in question, which leads to more effective learning, reflection and self-awareness. In order to make this intense form of coaching practical, long sessions should be avoided.

8. Opportunities to consult third parties

During coaching sessions, it is not customary to interrupt the dialogue to consult others. However, e-coaching makes it easier to pause the session to talk to third parties. The client can put the coach on hold (telephone) or turn off the camera (video) if they need to talk to a colleague or family member about their experiences or insights as part of the reflection process. The coach can also arrange breaks for reflection or intervision to support their own coaching strategy, although they must of course ensure that this is done in accordance with all applicable ethical standards. Due to its asynchronous nature, e-mail coaching offers the most opportunities to consult others.

The last seven ingredients apply to the types of e-coaching that uses the written word (i.e. chat and e-mail coaching).

9. Everything is in black and white

The frequent exchange of messages via chat and e-mail automatically ensure a clearly structured coaching programme. Normally, coaches make notes either during or after sessions, which they use to structure the coaching programme and monitor progress. However, with e-coaching, there is no need to take notes separately, as the entire communication process is recorded in black and white and saved for posterity. As a result, both the coach and the client can read over exactly what took place in the coaching process. This approach also makes it easier to refer back to earlier dialogue, to repeat things or to paraphrase specific thoughts, learning experiences and activities. The ability to review the subject matter also offers greater insight into the process.

10. Structure and motivation

Using the written word promotes the structure of the programme and the motivation of the client. The process of writing helps us to get our thoughts in order. Reading what we have written has an immediate personal impact and influences what you write next (instant reflection). This principle is known as the recursive process. Writing and reformulating our thoughts allows us to detach ourselves from our situation. From this objective point of view, we can clearly assess the situation and all associated thoughts and feelings. This facilitates learning and awareness, which in turn provides encouragement and motivation.

11. Reflective effect

Writing about a particular situation enables you to analyse it from the inside out via your computer screen. By distancing yourself from the problem in this way, you can view it from a variety of perspectives, re-evaluate the situation and put it in different contexts. The computer facilitates this process, effectively holding up a mirror and enabling detailed reflection. As the client types, their words instantly paint a written picture of their experiences. The more they write, the more objectively they can see their situation, which promotes therapeutic change.

12. Direct access to emotions

During written forms of e-coaching, the client reflects on his/her own actions, converting their thoughts into writing and simultaneously structuring these thoughts. This activates cognitive mechanisms that help the brain to process events on an emotional level. Writing about experiences and the associated emotions in the *first person present tense* gives you direct access to the emotions in question. This enables you to gain new insights into specific events and to relive the situation in order to help your brain process it. Emotions can also be activated via assignments that make use of symbols and pictures, enabling communication of these emotions (even for more sensitive issues). In an experiment with high school drop-outs, coaching via chat and e-mail was given with the aim of encouraging them to go back to school. To the amazement of the researchers, coaches and the youngsters themselves, this approach proved extremely successful. The youngsters who had difficulty talking about their emotions found it much easier to write about them. It gave them direct access to their emotions and enabled them to reflect. This experiment has been repeated successfully on numerous occasions.

13. Individual control of the process

The client has a large degree of autonomy, enabling them to decide for themselves where and when the coaching takes place. This creates a feeling of emotional control and comfort. In effect, e-coaching transfers control from the coach to the client. The client decides how often and how much they want to write (qualitative and quantitative), when to take breaks, whether to edit the text, add to it or delete parts of it. This promotes self-reliance and gives the client a very active and involved role in the coaching process.

14. Continuous positive reinforcement

Hope, optimism and positive expectations are widely regarded as the key factors in the effectiveness of coaching programmes. The coach must therefore gear the process towards achieving and maintaining this positivity. Chat and e-mail coaching greatly facilitates this. Research into e-mail coaching shows that e-mails containing positive words are more frequently read by the recipient and saved for longer periods. Coaches can capitalize upon this by sending positive and encouraging messages (recognition, compliments, positive feedback etc.) to the client in writing or adding motivational pictures. In addition to chat and e-mails, text messages (SMS) can also be used for this purpose. Because they are written down, the client can read the messages as many times as they please. This facilitates continual positive reinforcement and allows them to reread optimistic words in times of adversity. The messages can also be shared with third parties.

15. Regress prevention

Chat coaching and e-mail coaching create a written, tangible coproduction of a new way to view the world. By recording the coaching dialogue (consisting of all written text in the coaching programme), the client can review the coaching at a later date. After completion of the programme, rereading their self-written success story enables and encourages clients to maintain the positive changes they have made. Rereading is a valuable tool for measuring how far you have come and making the changes truly permanent. It also gives you clear insight into the coping mechanisms involved, which you can then use in future scenarios. In other words, if the client encounters similar difficulties in the future, they can immediately refer back to the coaching texts to see how they dealt with these situations during the coaching process. This prevents the client from lapsing back into old habits and hence makes coaching programmes truly sustainable.

4.2 The three pillars of e-coaching

The fifteen ingredients listed in the previous section are based on three vital elements, known as 'the three pillars of e-coaching'. The degree to which each pillar applies is dependent on the type of e-coaching. For e-mail coaching, all three process elements are involved (i.e. all fifteen ingredients are applicable). E-mail coaching therefore differs the most from F2F coaching, as illustrated in Table 2.1. The three pillars are:

1   Asynchronicity.
2   Social anonymity.
3   The written word.

4.2.1 Asynchronicity

In Chapter 2, we indicated that the aspect of time is an essential factor that varies according to the type of e-coaching used. In this respect, it refers to the time that elapses between communication exchanges, or in other words, the time taken for the coach to respond to a message from the client and vice versa. If the response is sent in little to no time, then it is referred to as synchronous communication. The communication is therefore conducted simultaneously. The longer the time between individual messages, the more asynchronous the communication. Within the field of communication studies, this term is primarily used to express the balance of power between two parties (equal standing is referred to as synchronous and non-equal standing as asynchronous). However, within the new discipline of CMC (see Section 3.1), the term 'synchronous' refers to the simultaneity of communication. By extension, asynchronicity means that the communication is not conducted simultaneously.

Synchronous communication is simultaneous, i.e. all parties are actively participating at the same time. The conversation is conducted by coach and client with little to no delay between the messages. The messages are sent via a computer with an Internet connection and the recipient of the message can respond almost instantaneously. This type of computer-aided communication is the most similar to a regular F2F conversation. Telephone, video and chat communication are all types of synchronous communication. The more time elapses before a response is sent, the less synchronous the communication.

Asynchronous communication is not simultaneous, i.e. it takes place at different times. The asynchronicity of the communication makes it time and location independent, as it does not matter where the coach or client are or when the communication takes place. Asynchronous communication is not a modern phenomenon. For example, smoke signals and blazing fire signals (fire beacons) are ancient methods of communication that sent messages across large distances without an immediate response being given. In his bestseller 'The Information: a history, a theory, a flood' the famous science writer James Gleick describes a fascinating and sophisticated way of asynchronous communication which was used by African Indian tribes: drum rumble. He writes: 'The drums generated fountains of oratory' and 'Here was a messaging system that outpaced the best couriers, the fastest horses on good roads with way stations and relays'.

A more modern form of asynchronous communication is letter writing, with letters being sent using carrier pigeons, carriages, boats, couriers etc. As a result, letters could take weeks, months or even years to reach their recipient. Nowadays, the technological developments in the field of CMC have reduced the delivery time to a fraction of a second. If the recipient responds straight away, we call it chat communication, while if a significant period of time elapses before a reply is given, then we call it e-mail communication. The Internet also offers other types of asynchronous communication such as Internet forums, where visitors to websites leave messages and respond to other people's messages (in the field of CMC, this is known as 'posting'). Countless websites offer this functionality, including LinkedIn, Facebook, MySpace and Pluform.

Non-written asynchronous communication

Asynchronous communication does not always have to be in written form. It is also possible to record audio or video messages that you can post online or send via e-mail. Voicemail messages are also a form of asynchronous communication, as the sender and recipient do not simultaneously participate in the communication.

Combining synchronicity and asynchronicity

Sometimes different types of e-coaching are thrown into the mix. Coaches can switch from synchronous to asynchronous communication or they can use a combination of both. An example of this is to send text messages. These are short messages (max. 160 characters) sent using a mobile phone. As the majority of people keep their mobile phone close to them practically at all times, you can often respond quickly. It is therefore similar to chat, although in general, the longer the message, the more time elapses before a reply is sent. If it takes a relatively long time, it is more like e-mail. Another highly popular program is WhatsApp. This is a smartphone application that has all of the characteristics of a chat program. When you send messages, the recipient's phone alerts them to the message so they can reply straight away. You can also see in real time whether the other person is typing a message. However, the recipient also knows that once they receive a message, they aren't necessarily expected to send a response immediately, as is the case in a chat session. As a result, WhatsApp can be used as either a chat or an e-mail program, so it is both synchronous and asynchronous. Nowadays, it is also possible to send text messages and to use programs like WhatsApp using a computer or other online device.

4.2.2 Social anonymity

Various studies into online therapy shows that anonymity is an important motivating factor in the decision to opt for online communication. In this section, we will explain why a certain degree of anonymity can help improve the structure and content of coaching programmes.

In the 1960s, the psychologist Robert Zajonc conducted a famous experiment that showed how people have more difficulty carrying out complex tasks in the presence of one or more people (an audience) compared to when they are alone. The explanation given for this is that the person experiences a physical reaction (tension, alertness) to the other person's presence and that they feel like they are being judged. The presence of an audience can therefore be detrimental to your ability to perform complex tasks. For more information about Zajonc's experiment, see the text box 'Spotlight: The Audience Effect' below.

Opening up during a coaching programme and attempting new behaviour are challenges that often prove difficult for clients. It is therefore perfectly logical that a great deal of a coach's training focuses on how to create a safe environment in which the client will feel at ease and hence be more willing to open up. They are also trained to appear non-judgmental, to keep a straight face and to avoid falling into the trap of countertransference. In most cases, clients will comply with social etiquette and display socially desirable behaviour. In effect, during F2F programmes, the coach and client assume a role that is largely dictated by the situation and interaction within the coaching programme. Coaching via e-mail or chat enables the coach and client to interact without actually meeting in the flesh, which creates social anonymity. With this type of anonymity, clients don't feel like they're being watched and they do not feel the need to observe the constraints of socially desirable behaviour. It also enables coaches to relax more and be themselves. They no longer have to concentrate on playing a certain role, and as such, the energy required to maintain that role can instead be focused on the issues at hand.

Spotlight: The Audience Effect

The psychologist Robert Zajonc is best known for his theory of social facilitation. This theory shows that people act differently in the presence of one or more people (an audience). Zajonc and a number of other researchers also showed that this effect applies not only to humans, but also other animals:

- ants have been shown to work six times harder in the presence of other ants compared to when they are alone,
- cockroaches get through easy mazes twice as fast – but complex mazes twice as slow – when in the presence of other cockroaches,
- chickens who stop feeding because they are full will start eating again if other chickens join them at the feed bowl.

Furthermore, Zajonc showed that people who had to perform complex tasks (such as learning new words or finding their way through a difficult maze) in the presence of others made more mistakes than when they tried to perform the tasks alone. He also showed that the reverse effect is true for easier tasks: people found simpler tasks easier when other people are present. The positive effect of an audience is known as 'social facilitation', while the negative effect of an audience is known as 'social inhibition'. One explanation for these phenomena is that the presence of others triggers a response in the body (e.g. fear of being judged). This tension helps you to perform simple tasks, but makes it harder to perform complex tasks. This tension results in measurable physical responses, such as an increase in heart rate or perspiration.

An amusing study by ethologist Melissa Bateson tested this effect, but instead of other people, the 'audience' consisted merely of a large poster featuring two eyes that appeared to stare at you. The poster was placed in the coffee corner in a canteen, together with an 'honesty box' in which people could put money to pay for their coffee.

When the poster featuring the eyes was placed above the honesty box, people were 2.7 times more likely to pay for their coffee in comparison to when the poster was not there. Once we feel or think we are being watched, we act differently!

The psychological functions of social anonymity

Three functions of social anonymity are defined in scientific literature (Pederson, 1997; Croes, 2010):

1 Recovery.
2 Disclosure.
3 Autonomy.

The *recovery function* relates to the phenomenon of 'disinhibition', i.e. the opportunity to reduce the inhibition process. Inhibition is the restraint or avoidance of negative emotions and the suppression of thoughts. This can result in increasing physiological tension (such as perspiration or an increase in heart rate/blood pressure) and negative moods. Disinhibition is the process of reducing this suppression of emotions and thoughts. The recovery function relates to how you need an opportunity for release after, for example, leaving a meeting during which you had to suppress particular emotions. The same factor applies to all social situations in which inhibition is a factor. Release is possible in a familiar environment or in an environment in which people can be themselves, without the obligation to display socially desirable behaviour.

Disclosure is the process of opening up to another person, confiding personal information about yourself or a certain situation in your life. It is the uninhibited expression of thoughts and feelings without shame or fear of judgment. This is a basic human need, but social conventions mean that it can be difficult to realize. However, it is much easier when there is a degree of anonymity, such as talking to a stranger who you will probably never meet again or visiting a website where you can post anonymous messages (such as sharesecrets.org, www.secretsanon.com etc.)

Autonomy relates to how capable a person is of deciding for him/herself what to do or not to do. In other words, it relates to how free someone is. Being able to act autonomously is a basic human need. It is important to be an independent person with a large degree of control over your own behaviour and body. Anonymity means that people are less able to control you. The more autonomous you are, the more freedom you have to experiment with new behaviour without worrying about possible social consequences or negative reactions. Becoming dependent on a coach takes away the autonomy of the client and can compromise the coaching process. One of the ultimate goals of every coaching programme is to make the coach's job redundant.

Success factors of social anonymity within e-coaching

The three aforementioned functions of social anonymity have a positive effect on an individual's psychological well-being. With e-mail coaching, the coach's lack of physical presence ensures maximum social anonymity during the coaching process.

The venting of emotions relating to particular experiences or events is an important part of the client's dialogue. Emotions can be freely expressed without fearing negative and/or disapproving reactions. This reduces social inhibition and shame and encourages openness, candour and intimacy, which makes it easier to discuss taboo subjects. In everyday situations, aspects of physical appearance play a role in how people interact. With asynchronous communication, there is less chance of developing such prejudices as you cannot see the person you are talking to and any physical clues are hidden. Due to the lack of physical aspects, the parties are not distracted by superficial matters and can get straight to the point, focusing purely on the client's coaching objective. Online communication gives both parties a voice but liberates them from stereotyping. As the client doesn't have to worry about their appearance and presentation, and hence how the other person will judge them, it is easier for them to open up. However, it is important to note that the lack of visual presence eliminates non-verbal communication, which can result in misunderstandings. It is therefore important that extra care and attention is given to avoiding such misconceptions.

Being in their home or work environment gives the client a feeling of familiarity and invisibility. They don't feel like they're being watched or judged. This gives them a feeling of immunity as they can get out at any time with no questions asked and no need to explain themselves. All of these factors provide a great sense of security, encouraging clients to reveal more about themselves and to explore hidden aspects of their personality.

4.2.3 The written word

Another way of distinguishing the various types of e-coaching is to categorize them according to the means of expression used. This classification relates to whether the communication is in spoken or written form. F2F coaching is predominantly based on spoken dialogue, which makes telephone and video coaching the most similar e-coaching methods to traditional F2F coaching. However, modern coaching programmes are increasingly making use of the written word via chat and e-mail coaching. These media have become extremely important due to the increasing influence that computers and the Internet have on our everyday lives. Various studies into digital services have shown that the popularity of communication via the written word is rising quicker than any other medium. Other studies conducted into the therapy profession have shown that e-therapy, e-mail consultations and other types of text-based communication can yield excellent results. The crucial factor when using this type of written communication is to be extremely careful and deliberate in your language use. This means that all responses and feedback must be very carefully formulated, especially those sent by the coach. In Chapter 6, we will discuss how the coach can use linguistic analysis and strategies in order to optimize this type of communication.

Why write?

The psychologist James Pennebaker once conducted a study in which subjects were asked to write about a past trauma. The results showed that far more positive changes had been achieved than had been expected. These changes related to social and linguistic behaviour. The experiment showed that people who wrote about their traumas were able to talk more openly about them with others, they smiled and laughed more, and they changed their network of friends (they stopped associating with certain people and welcomed new friends into their network). For more information about this study, see the text box 'Spotlight: The Expressive Writing Paradigm'.

This experiment has been repeated many times by other researchers, who all realized similar results. In summary, writing about traumatic events helps the brain to process them cognitively and emotionally. First, an *immediate cognitive change* takes place as the writer has to linguistically formulate the information about the trauma, which cognitively structures and organizes the trauma. Second, an *immediate emotional change* takes place, as being confronted with an emotional event often triggers coping and elimination processes. Furthermore, lasting social changes are realized in addition to cognitive and emotional changes. In regular coaching programmes, written exercises are used very frequently, and e-coaching takes this even further, with e-mail and chat used as the default means of expression.

Spotlight: The Expressive Writing Paradigm

The following is a description of the original experiment that demonstrates the power of writing. As part of the study, all participants were asked to write for 20–30 minutes, once a day, for a period of three days. The experimental group was asked to write about a particular past trauma and describe their deepest thoughts and feelings associated with this event. Meanwhile, the control group was asked to write for the same amount of time about a superficial topic. The results of this simple written intervention proved significant: subjects in the experimental group visited their doctor less frequently than the subjects in the control group. Various biomedical examinations also showed that in comparison to the control group, the experimental subjects displayed significant improvement regarding the function of their immune system, hormonal activity and other biological indicators of stress or illness, including their behaviour.

Written interventions are a useful phenomenon because they can be implemented quickly and cheaply. Furthermore, studies show that the writing process can have positive effects after just three exercises, and in some cases even after as few as one.

Success factors of writing

Writing and reformulating problems – and hence simultaneously structuring your problems, thoughts and emotions in your mind – have a motivational effect. Expunging the past from your memory has a powerful therapeutic effect. Consistent and significant improvements in health and well-being have been shown to occur in individuals as soon as they start to write about past traumas. Writing is therapeutically effective as it is liberating and helps unburden the mind. It helps clients to intensively and intently examine their inner self and their environment, which in turn allows them to see relevant situations and experiences from a different perspective. It mobilizes the client's inner strength and independence. Writing is associated with improvements in insight, self-reflection, optimism, self-esteem and a sense of control. The therapeutic effectiveness of writing is attributed to the fact that clients can express themselves freely to promote order and clarity in their mind. The health benefits of writing relate not only to the release of repressed negative emotions, but also to the increased understanding of your true self and feelings.

Two underlying explanations for why writing helps improve health are the functions of inhibition and disclosure. Both have been described in the section about social anonymity. Writing enables you to freely express your inner thoughts and emotions. Because you no longer need to hold back, your stress levels are reduced, which promotes physiological and psychological well-being. Clients have also reported that they benefit not only from letting go of repressed emotions, but also that the writing gives them greater insight into the things that distress them. Another explanation is the *self-regulation theory*, which asserts that writing allows people to effectively observe themselves whilst expressing and controlling their emotions. The client therefore feels more capable of controlling their stressors, which reduces negative thoughts and improves general well-being.

4.3 Summary

In this chapter, we described all of the important ingredients that facilitate and accelerate the e-coaching process. In total, there are fifteen key aspects, of which the first eight apply to all types of e-coaching. These universal aspects of e-coaching are as follows:

1   Location and time independence (the coaching can take place 24/7, assuming access to a computer and Internet connection).
2   Frequent contact (the lack of travelling time makes it easier to schedule more sessions in a small space of time).
3   Baby steps (more frequent contact opportunities allow you to split the coaching into bite-size chunks, increasing the chances of success).
4   On-the-job learning (the coaching takes place in familiar surroundings, so the client conducts the process in a real-life setting).
5   High level of engagement (the frequent contact and increased number of successes promotes increased engagement).
6   Straight to the point (by eliminating the need for social chat and socially desirable behaviour, greater attention can be paid to the issues at hand).
7   Optimal focus (the communication method enables better concentration).
8   Opportunities to consult third parties (consulting others is possible without interrupting the coaching session).

The other seven aspects relate to communication via the written word. They are therefore only applicable to chat and e-mail coaching. These aspects are:

9   Everything is in black and white (words cannot 'evaporate' – as they are recorded, they are set in stone).
10 Structure and motivation (the writing process automatically creates order and structure in the client's thoughts and emotions).
11 Reflective effect (via the screen, clients are immediately confronted with what they have written).
12 Direct access to emotions (the writing process activates the emotional system).
13 Individual control of the process (clients are free to decide when to communicate and are actively involved in the coaching process).
14 Continuous positive reinforcement (positive messages can be saved and reread).
15 Regress prevention (completed coaching programmes can be repeatedly reviewed).

The more similar the type of e-coaching is to F2F coaching, the fewer ingredients apply to it. All of these aspects apply to e-mail coaching, making this type the most dissimilar to F2F. The fifteen aspects are based on three key elements: asynchronicity, social anonymity and the written word. We refer to these elements as the three pillars of effective e-coaching. Asynchronicity enables both coach and client to decide when to participate in the coaching process. The opportunity for frequent contact enables the programme to be divided into bite-size chunks, which results in more moments of triumph for the client. The amount of time for reflection is also increased. Social anonymity allows the client to work on their coaching objectives in familiar, safe environments and relieves them of the obligation to behave in a socially desirable manner. As a result, there is a significant reduction in shame and social inhibition, which makes it easier to get straight to the heart of the matter. The third pillar is the written word. Studies have shown the healing power of the written word and how it facilitates the processing of traumatic events. By conducting the coaching process in writing, the entire dialogue is recorded. This enables clients to reread everything they've learned during the coaching process at their leisure.

In order to optimally implement these three process elements into the coaching process, we have developed a new coaching model, which we will present in Chapter 5. Furthermore, in Part II of the book, we will show how this model can be put into practice.

5

THE ABC MODEL FOR ACTUAL CHANGE

In the previous chapters, we described the different types of e-coaching. We also discussed the active ingredients that contribute to its success, a number of which are also found in F2F coaching. After all, e-coaching is not a completely new type of coaching, simply a modernized version with significantly different dynamics and intensity. Each type of e-coaching requires coaches to adopt a different approach and learn a new set of skills. To help coaches on their way, we have developed a model that lays the groundwork for e-coaching programmes. This model specifically accommodates the way people learn and realize behavioural change. In this chapter, we will present the ABC model and illustrate how it can be applied within the field of e-coaching.

5.1 Development of the ABC model

ABC stands for *Accelerated Behavioural Change*. As the name suggests, it provides a structure for realizing lasting changes in behaviour in a short space of time. The model consists of three main stages: *Analyse, Internalize and Sustain*. The first stage involves investigation and introspection, the second stage consists of implementing the new behaviour in your everyday life, and the final stage relates to maintenance and preservation of your new skills and behaviour. Coaching programmes can be conducted via these three stages, with specific steps being taken as part of each separate stage.

A classic basic model

Graham Alexander's famous GROW model is the inspiration for the Analyse stage (the first stage of the ABC model). GROW stands for *Goal, Reality, Options, Wrap up*, or in other words, set a goal, examine where you currently stand in relation to this goal, assess which options and tools are available to you, and get to work. The GROW model provides an effective basic structure for coaching programmes and is particularly useful for newly qualified coaches. Over the years, however, the model has attracted criticism. Some say it is too simplistic, others say that it lacks certain essential aspects of coaching. As a result, a myriad of alternative models have been developed with catchy acronyms such as ACHIEVE, SUCCESS and DESIRE. However, further scrutiny of these models nearly always shows that they are little more than extensions of Graham Alexander's basic model. At first, Alexander himself didn't realize that his coaching consisted of four stages, and had to be informed of this by outsiders. They told him that his coaching featured certain aspects that had already been recognized within the field of psychology (including the *goal-setting theory*). Alexander subsequently studied these aspects in collaboration with early Inner Gamers and McKinsey & Company and adopted the terms in order to develop his own model. We used the same approach when developing the ABC model. We studied the methods of countless coaches and drew inspiration from a wide range of knowledge in the fields of social psychology, cognitive behavioural therapy and developmental psychology. We then condensed this wealth of information into a model that optimally accommodates the way coachees learn new behaviour.

New insights into behavioural development

The belief that people cannot change is a frequently held misconception. It is reinforced by the fact that many behavioural interventions ignore the specific opportunities and obstacles that help or hinder positive change in the client. The ABC model has been developed in order to take full advantage of the client's opportunities (i.e. intrinsic motivation, cognition) and to accommodate the client's limitations (i.e. beliefs, environment, time, support). A recent study by Stanford University shows that a frequently made mistake is 'trying to take big leaps instead of baby steps'. By attempting these big leaps, the number of 'victories' declines, which harms the client's motivation and makes them more likely to throw in the towel. Motivation is a fundamental condition for achieving enduring behavioural change. See also Section 4.1, item 3: Baby steps.

Another typical problem with interventions is the *transfer of coaching*. This is the degree to which the client applies their newly acquired knowledge, skills and behaviour in their work and/or private life. For interpersonal skills training, the transfer is rarely higher than 20 per cent. In other words, just 20 per cent of what clients learn is actually put into practice. To a great degree, this extremely low percentage is mainly due to the fact that the new behaviour and skills are learned in fictitious situations (see Section 4.1, item 4: On the job learning). Training and coaching programmes focus strongly on learning and practicing new behaviour (frequently making use of role plays and actors). However, the clients only find out if their new behaviour is practically applicable and useful when they try it out in everyday scenarios. The phrase 'the proof of the pudding is in the eating' is particularly applicable here. A new phenomenon is *on-the-job coaching*. This involves the coach travelling to their client's workplace in order to better assist them in implementing their new skills and behaviour. This makes the coaching much more relevant to the client, although it is very costly. Furthermore, the presence of an outsider in the workplace can be disruptive. As a result, there are question marks regarding how popular this type of coaching will become.

The aforementioned insights are the foundations upon which the ABC model was built. In the first stage of the ABC model, time is taken to formulate realistic, relevant and achievable goals. In the second stage, the client works on achieving these goals. The two key aspects of stage 2 are that the goals are split into concrete, clearly formulated subgoals which are realized by taking *baby steps*, and that a relevant environment is identified in which the client can take them. During these steps, the client will receive continual positive reinforcement from both the coach and the environment (e.g. the workplace or home environment). This will result in a greater number of successes, which in turn encourages the client to display the new skills and behaviour more often. This combination of factors results in greater, quicker and more enduring behavioural change.

5.2 The Accelerated Behavioural Change model in detail

5.2.1 Three stages and three core elements

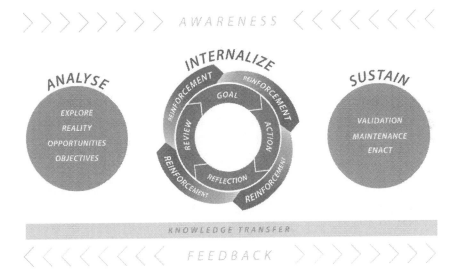

FIGURE 5.1 The ABC model
Source: © Ribbers and Waringa (2011)

The ABC model consists of three main stages, each consisting of a number of substages. The main stages are *Analyse, Internalize and Sustain.* In addition to these three stages, the model also features three process elements: *Awareness, Feedback* and *Knowledge transfer.* These elements are featured in all coaching programmes, although the degree to which they apply depends on the type of programme and the coaching objective in question. We will now discuss the various stages and process elements in detail.

5.2.2 Phase 1: Analyse – input phase

Phase 1: Analyse

The first stage of the model is the analysis stage. This stage is very similar to the GROW model and the first stage of many other coaching methods. The goal of the first stage is to paint a picture of the client's current situation: establish the client's view of his/her situation, list all of the opportunities available and determine the desired situation (the goals that are achievable within the coaching programme). This stage has a linear structure, and the coaching objective is analysed based on the following four steps: *Explore, Reality, Opportunities and Objectives.*

1 *Explore:* During the exploratory stage, the coaching objective is examined and approached from a variety of perspectives. All important information about the client's current situation is identified and discussed. A number of tools can be used to assist this process, such as writing a biography, asking targeted questions, completing specific accredited tests, conducting assessments or offering exploratory assignments. You can also involve other people from the client's life to help in the process, e.g. via a 360 degree instrument.

2 *Reality:* During this step, the coach and client investigate how the client interprets the information from step 1 and relates it to their situation. In other words, where does the client believe he/she stands regarding the matter at hand, and upon what underlying convictions (assumptions) is this perspective based? Here, the client must distinguish between assumptions, emotions and facts. By asking open-ended questions, you allow the client to formulate a detailed description of their current situation. In this stage, the original coaching issue is expanded upon and linked to the current context, behaviour and convictions.

During this stage, you can also identify any elements that help maintain the status quo and what the consequences (both advantages and disadvantages) would be if the situation did not change. A characteristic feature of this stage is the breakthrough that the client experiences when the 'question behind the question' is discovered. Until this point is reached, the coaching can only treat the symptoms, leaving the core issues untouched. Once the client realizes and accepts what lies at the core of their coaching objective, then the next phase can begin.

3   *Opportunities:* During this step, we consider the desired situation and why it is important to the client to achieve it. Subsequently, a road map is drawn up illustrating how the client can get from the current situation to the desired situation. In this step, you can again make use of open-ended questions to create a detailed picture of the desired situation (one example of a technique that can be used here is the 'ideal situation'').You can then identify everything available to the client in order to make this new situation a reality. What options are open to the client in order to realize change? What is necessary to achieve it (e.g. knowledge, skills, support, money, time)? Who is essential to the process? (Who is/could be involved in the process?) It is up to the client to identify all of these aspects (self-discovery). This process can be accelerated and reinforced by encouraging the client to think *outside of the box*, e.g. by imagining him/herself in the place of somebody who is already in the desired situation. A recent study indicated that strength-based approaches are the most effective, i.e. focusing on the opportunities available to clients rather than on clients' limitations.

4   *Objectives:* In the final step of stage 1, a number of clearly defined and achievable objectives are formulated. These objectives will be the leading factor in the next two stages of the coaching programme. Eventually, these objectives will be used to assess whether the coaching programme has achieved the predetermined goals. In order to ensure realistic objectives, it is important to identify which obstacles and limitations could hinder the client's progress. One methodology that can help ensure concrete objectives is the SMART system (Specific, Measurable, Acceptable, Realistic, Time-bound).[2] Another technique is using rating scale questions, where the client is asked to award each of their relevant skills a score of between 1 and 10.

5.2.3 Phase 2: Internalize – the client circle and the reinforcement circle

Phase 2: Internalize

The internalization stage is the most distinctive stage of the ABC model in comparison to other coaching models. The difference is apparent in both the structure and the execution. It is the practical stage of the model and consists of two process circles. One process circle contains the active positive reinforcement provided by both the coach and the client's environment, while the other circle displays the cycle of four steps that the client repeats as many times as is required.

The client circle

In the second stage, the client will proactively work on his points for development. This is about acquiring and internalizing new skills and/or behaviours necessary to achieve the desired objectives (determined in the previous stage). In order to do this, the client will repeatedly conduct the four cyclical process steps (*Goal, Action, Reflection, Review*) under the continual guidance of the coach. The steps will be repeated as often as it takes for the client to realize and internalize true behavioural change. It is an iterative process, achieving results by repeatedly running through the process. This stage also involves short process steps ('baby steps'), frequent contact with the coach, regular reflection, daily practice in a relevant environment and lots of feedback. The four cyclical steps that the client will repeat are:

1   *Goal:* A goal is an operationalized *objective* from stage 1. These goals relate to a particular desired situation (a particular skill or behaviour). Once you divide the goals into subgoals, you can formulate specific exercises or assignments (behavioural experiments) for each subgoal, which the client can then carry out in a practical environment (e.g. at home or at work). Here, it is important to identify the desired consequences stemming from these goals, the obstacles that the client may encounter (how likely are they and how can they be overcome?) and the point at which an assignment or exercise can be said to have been successfully completed. If desired, the SMART technique or rating scale questions can be used again. You can also use a specific type of scale question known as the GAS (*Goal Attainment Scaling*) method, in which the importance (desirability) and the difficulty level of the goals/subgoals can be assessed.

2   *Action:* In this step, the client actively works towards achieving the goals/subgoals formulated in step 1. In this stage, the client puts all of their ideas, expectations and good intentions into action by carrying out exercises and assignments. Recent research has shown that people's behaviour is significantly influenced by the environment and/or situation in which they find themselves. As a result, it is necessary to conduct the exercises and assignments in a practical situation that is realistic and relevant to the client. By conducting the assignments on-the-job or in the client's home environment, a real-life situation is created featuring real experiences. The more realistic and small-scale an exercise is, the more moments of success the client will experience.

3   *Reflection:* The purpose of the third step is to help the client interpret and perpetuate the experiences gained in the previous step. The client's experiences regarding their own behaviour, the reactions of the people around them (other relevant parties, if present) and the results achieved must be recorded as soon as possible. Answers to the following questions must be obtained: What exactly happened? What happened next? What emotions were triggered? By recording all of this information, preferably as soon as possible after the event so the emotions are still fresh in the mind, the client gains extra

insight into the opportunities that this new behaviour offers. This type of on-the-job learning greatly facilitates the transfer of coaching and increases the chances of realizing enduring behavioural change.

4   *Review:* After the reflection process, the client reviews and contemplates what they have learned and experienced. How do they look back on the experience and what effect has it had (in a variety of areas)? Have the desired results been achieved or not? During every review moment, a decision can be made about whether to repeat the experiment or not, whether to fine-tune it, whether to increase the difficulty level or whether to conduct a related assignment. In principle, this process can be repeated as many times as is necessary to achieve the desired results. Once these results have been achieved, you can decide whether to work on a different goal/subgoal from the previous stage or whether to continue to stage 3.

The reinforcement circle

The surrounding reinforcement circle supports the client's process circle. This process circle represents how both the coach and the client's environment can continually structure, support, encourage and positively reinforce the client's progress. This stage helps to embed everything the client has learned by means of the reinforcement principle. Reinforcement ensures that specific behaviour in particular situations is encouraged or discouraged by associating the behaviour with positive or negative consequences (also known as operant conditioning). This type of learning follows the principle that rewarded behaviour will be repeated more often, while unrewarded or punished behaviour will be extinguished. In situations where the client is trying new behaviour or skills, a form of reinforcement will always occur, originating from the situation or environment. Furthermore, the coach can actively make targeted use of reinforcement in order to encourage the client's progress.

- *Environmental reinforcement:* By carrying out exercises (behavioural experiments) in a practical setting, the client will get a reaction from his environment. If the new behaviour is received positively, it will give positive reinforcement to the newly learned behaviour. If the client experiments with new behaviour and does not receive a positive response that can indicate that there is still room for improvement. If the lack of positive response persists, then the client's behaviour is negatively reinforced. In order to prevent negative reinforcement, it is important that during the first step (Goal), a clear picture is created of what the desired positive situation is and what behaviour is required in order to realize it.
- *Reinforcement by the coach:* Via brief messages, positive feedback, compliments and encouragement, the coach can encourage the client to perform the behavioural experiments effectively and to learn from the experiences gained. By showing approval, commitment and recognition, the coach helps positively

reinforce the client's behaviour and help them to internalize what they have learned. The coach must also play another role, i.e. intervening in the event of possible misinterpretations or faulty assumptions that stem from negative consequences experienced by the client. For example, if a client has a bad experience, then the coach can reassure them and help paint a rosier picture of what the actual consequences are. In this way, the coach can prevent possible negative reinforcement.

By using the reinforcement principle at every opportunity throughout the internalization stage, the coach can accelerate the client's progress and hence also the entire coaching process.

5.2.4 Phase 3: Sustain – output phase

Phase 3: Sustain

To be certain that the objectives formulated in stage 1 are achieved and endure into the future, the final stage focuses on the sustainability of the coaching process. If the process has been conducted effectively and a large degree of internalization has been effectuated, then the final stage will only take a short time. This stage consists of the following three steps:

1   *Validation:* In this step, the newly developed and internalized behaviour (and any other objectives achieved) will be validated. Here, the coach and client will assess to what extent the client has realized and internalized the objectives they set. By clearly formulating the objectives in the first stage, the coach and client can then share their opinions and enable optimal feedback. A more objective form of validation is the use of accredited questionnaires or scale questions in both the first and last stages of the coaching process. Another possible technique is by asking the opinions of the people directly involved in the client's everyday life. This can gauge whether the client's behavioural changes were noticeable to others. Once agreement has been reached about the results achieved, you can continue to the next step.
2   *Maintenance:* This step is about preserving the results achieved in the previous step. In principle, the client him/herself is capable of maintaining the results thanks to the internalization stage. However, the client and coach can also work on a number of tools that they can use should they ever need to brush up on what they learned. The client can draw up a list of all of the learning experiences gained that paved the way to the end results. This list can be displayed in a table, and for each learning experience, the client can note down

what behaviour related to what experience and how this behaviour came about (e.g. what was the situation, which skills did you use, did you have help from anyone, were particular resources used?) Based on these findings, the coach and client can investigate how the new behaviour can be continued, safeguarded and expanded upon. In principle, all of the answers to these questions can be found in this table, as it will contain all of the ingredients that were required to realize this behaviour. By focusing on these ingredients, it is possible to reproduce the behaviour in future. In order to expand on this behavioural change (even further than the predetermined situations), it is possible to create a list of additional strategies (e.g. who or what are necessary in order to expand on this behaviour). This principle is based on appreciative and solution-focused coaching methods (i.e. do what works).

3   *Enact:* In the final step, the client takes the baton and perpetuates their new skills and behaviour into the future. Thanks to the previous step, the client now has a clear overview of the behaviour they wish to continue and maintain in the long term and how to do this. By working independently on this in their own lives, the coaching programme has an enduring effect. Finally, the client can agree to send e-mail updates after a set amount of time to let the coach know how they are getting on. The coach can also take the initiative, sending an e-mail after a period of time to ask how the client is doing.

5.2.5 Three process elements: Awareness/Feedback/Knowledge transfer

The coaching process involves a number of process elements that enable the client to make the necessary steps. They form the basis for the work that will be done. These three elements are:

1   *Awareness:* It is essential to the process that the client discovers and develops self-awareness. This is classified as a process element because it features in many of the steps involved in the three main stages. It is an indispensable ingredient of the personal development process. Awareness can be described as the subjective reflection on stimuli from the outside world (knowing what you see, hear or feel and being able to talk about it) or on your own mental processes (knowing what is happening in your head and being able to talk about it). In other words, awareness is a state of mind characterized by consciousness of your own self in your interactions with the world around you. Within the coaching process, clients will become increasingly aware of their own behaviour and convictions in certain situations. The clients' awareness of their own values will also be increased: How do I derive meaning? What are my strengths and weaknesses? What is the greatest challenge in the course of my development? Gaining awareness is a continual process that is not merely confined to one particular stage, step or goal, but plays a major role on numerous occasions throughout the entire process.

2   *Feedback:* This is another essential element in every form of coaching. Giving feedback is one of the most important skills for a coach to have. Feedback allows the coach and client to share information about each other's experiences, attitudes and behaviour. This is one of the main factors that allows clients to critically examine their actions and make changes if necessary. Feedback plays a major role in every stage and every step in the ABC model. Frequent feedback enables accelerated progress, particularly in stage 2 (Internalize).

3   *Knowledge transfer:* Throughout the entire process, a great deal of knowledge and information is shared in a structured manner. At various moments in the coaching process, it can be useful to offer the client background information in order to give the programme more depth or to help the client gain important insights. This information can come in a variety of forms, such as articles about particular subjects, diagrams of models, specific tests, videos showing example situations or additional explanation to help with an assignment. This information could be sourced from the coach's own library or the coach may have searched for it somewhere else especially for that particular coaching programme. The amount of extra information required depends on the needs of the client and can therefore be flexibly distributed regardless of which stage the coaching process is at. The provision of structured information within the coaching process is a method taken from the therapy profession (where it is known as psychoeducation).

5.3 E-coaching based on the ABC model

The ABC model is optimally compatible with how people learn and realize behavioural change. Thanks to the generic first stage, this model can be flexibly applied in accordance with the guidelines of any coaching method, including:

- Solution-oriented coaching.
- Development-oriented coaching.
- Socratic coaching.
- Strength-based coaching.
- Co-active coaching.
- Cognitive behavioural coaching.
- Systematic coaching.
- NLP coaching.
- Voice dialogue.

Theoretically, the ABC model can be used as a basis for any coaching programme. However, in practice, it doesn't work very well for F2F coaching. This is because it is generally not possible to take small developmental steps in F2F due to scheduling issues and high costs. An average coaching programme consists of a series of periodic meetings every two or three weeks. In the intervening time, the client may carry out individual assignments and exercises, but the feedback on these assignments has to wait until the next meeting. Due to the considerable amount of time between the meetings, the assignments are usually very large so the client can make maximum use of the available time. Smaller steps would therefore require an increase in the frequency of meetings to enable relevant feedback and reflection on these smaller assignments. Due to the scheduling problems this would create and the travelling time/costs for both coach and client, it is not feasible to conduct F2F coaching in this way. However, this method is perfectly compatible with e-coaching, as the ABC model perfectly accommodates its key aspects. By making efficient use of the Internet, it is possible to greatly increase the frequency of contact moments. The coaching programme can therefore be split into smaller, bite-size chunks. The increased frequency of contact really comes into its own in stage 2. In this stage, the client is frequently experimenting with new behaviour, trying things out and practicing new skills in a relevant context with continual guidance from the coach. This significantly accelerates the process of behavioural change. Depending on the type of e-coaching used, other elements can also contribute to the successful application of the ABC model. E-mail coaching, for example, includes all three process amplifiers (asynchronicity, social anonymity and written communication), which further accelerates behavioural change.

Finally, the ABC model and the accompanying technological applications are compatible with nearly all types of coaching programme. One exception is coaching that involves activities that cannot be digitalized, such as body-oriented coaching, equine assisted coaching, coaching during walks or coaching on a boat. However, due to the rapid developments in the field of virtual reality and gaming technology (such as the Nintendo Wii), even these types of activities may be digitally reproducible in the future. In any case, it is still possible to support these types of physical and/or outdoor coaching with elements of e-coaching.

5.4 Summary

In this chapter, we have introduced a new coaching model known as the Accelerated Behavioural Change (ABC) model. It is specifically compatible with e-coaching as it was specially designed for behavioural interventions that make use of the Internet. The ABC model consists of three stages: Analyse, Internalize and Sustain. The first stage of the model is about defining the coaching objectives, and consists of four steps: Explore (what do I want to achieve?), Reality (what is my current situation and how does it differ from my desired situation?), Opportunities (what options are open to me in relation to achieving my goals?) and Objectives (what are my clearly defined goals?) This stage is similar to the well-known GROW model. The most distinctive stage of e-coaching is stage 2: Internalize. This consists of two process circles: a client circle with the four cyclical steps Goal, Action, Reflection and Review, and a reinforcement circle representing the positive reinforcement provided by the coach and the client's environment. During this stage, the client works on implementing new behaviour in a real-life setting with the coach providing intensive guidance. The client makes small steps and therefore experiences more moments of triumph along the way, which contributes to the development and internalization of new behaviour. Both the client's environment and the coach positively reinforce the successes experienced. The final stage (Sustain) is used to make the new knowledge, skills and behaviour a permanent fixture in the client's life. This stage consists of three steps: Validation (evaluating whether the main objectives have been achieved), Maintenance (creating plans that help sustain the new behaviour) and Enact (perpetuating the new knowledge and behaviour without the coach's assistance). Finally, the ABC model involves three process elements that are almost constantly in play during the coaching process. These process elements are: Awareness (the client gains increasing insight into their own behaviour and the environment in which that behaviour manifests itself), Feedback (continual communication with the coach to help shape the client's behaviour and the coaching process in general) and Knowledge transfer (provision of background information to the client).

The ABC model enables the application of a wide range of methods and techniques, and predominantly serves as a guideline for the coaching process. Every e-coaching programme can be conducted in accordance with this model. The main challenge for the coach is learning the skills necessary to conduct effective e-coaching, particularly e-mail coaching. Changing from F2F coaching to e-mail coaching involves a switch from verbal to written communication, introduces the aspect of asynchronicity and geographically separates the coach and client. As a result, the coach must learn new skills in order to ensure clear communication and develop a good online coach–client relationship. In addition to the ABC model, we have also developed a new method to help coaches develop the skills necessary for e-mail coaching, known as the eCoachPro method. In the following chapter, we will discuss this new method and in Part II we will show you how to apply it in practice.

Notes

1   The 'ideal situation' is a frequently used coaching tool to help the client describe how they would like their life to be with regard to the coaching objective and what consequences this would have. The following is an example of such a question: 'Imagine you woke up tomorrow and your ideal situation had suddenly become reality. How would you know?'

2   Within the GROW model, Graham Alexander uses a slightly different definition of SMART: Specific, Measurable, Achievable, Relevant and Trackable.

6

THE ECOACHPRO METHOD FOR ONLINE TEXT-BASED COACHING

In Chapter 3 and 4, we discussed in detail the effects of e-communication on the coaching process. The visibility (or lack thereof) of the conversation partner, the (a)synchronous presence in the conversation and the use of the written word all have an effect on how the parties interact. Practically all studies conducted into the effect of coaching have shown that the professional relationship between coach and client is a decisive factor in the success of the programme. To a great extent, this relationship is shaped by the way in which the two parties communicate. It goes without saying that depending on the type of e-coaching, there are a variety of ways in which the professional relationship can be shaped.

The communication within e-mail coaching differs the most from F2F coaching (see Table 2.1). The eCoachPro (eCP) method was specifically developed for the purposes of text-based (e-mail) coaching, in which writing is the predominant means of expression. The eCP method helps the coach to communicate effectively and build up a relationship with the client. It also enables structural analysis of the client's messages. In this chapter, we will explain the theoretical background of the eCP method and address linguistic strategies, text analysis, speech acts and efficient use of language. Subsequently, in Part II of the book, we will describe in detail the practical application of the eCP method, explaining the two processes and the various steps involved and including concrete examples.

6.1 The coach–client relationship

At the start of an F2F coaching programme, the foundations of a professional relationship are laid, and the all-important click is established between coach and client. As the coaching progresses, the relationship is maintained and built upon. With chat or e-mail coaching where no F2F intake is conducted, there is no obvious phase in which the relationship is built up, and it can be more difficult to achieve a click between coach and client. With e-mail coaching, because the process takes place online, there is a degree of social anonymity. On the one hand, this helps the client get to the heart of the matter more quickly, but on the other hand, the relationship and the mutual trust take longer to build up compared to F2F coaching. Working online means that the parties cannot really get a feel for each other in order to build up a social bond of trust. A large amount of information is also missing: you may not know the gender, age, name etc. of the person you are talking to, which can make the communication feel stiff and impersonal. Furthermore, the lack of visibility frequently results in both parties creating unrealistic or idealistic assumptions about the other with regard to identity, appearance etc. This can have a beneficial effect on the coaching process, although it can just as easily disrupt it.

Chat and e-mail communication can sometimes be tricky due to the coach and client misunderstanding each other. This is due to the omission of certain information. For example, there is less context that can clarify the meaning behind certain messages. The majority of the non-verbal communication is eliminated, decreasing the feeling of connection and increasing the likelihood of misunderstandings. The information is interpreted based on the listener's own frame of reference, so misinterpretations occur more frequently. Studies show, for example, that during online dialogue, clients often feel like the coach has difficulty understanding them.

In Chapter 3, we gave a detailed description of the pros and cons of e-communication. However, the advantages mentioned – such as reduced inhibition, greater openness, greater equality, extra time for reflection and increased personal control over the process – do not come automatically. Realization of these advantages depends on the attitude between the coach and client during the coaching process. At first, it is the coach's responsibility to ensure that the communication facilitates the creation of a stable professional relationship that maximizes the advantages of e-coaching and minimizes the disadvantages. To help coaches establish a good relationship with their clients, we developed the eCoachPro (eCP) method. By applying this method in combination with the ABC model, coaches can create, structure and conduct effective e-coaching programs to realize enduring behavioural change. Written messages form the basis of e-mail coaching. As the written word is used to develop the coach–client relationship, the eCP method is based on insights, theories and strategies from the field of linguistics.

6.2 Politeness theory: the heart of the eCP method

The most important coaching instrument is the *dialogue* between coach and client. Language allows us to communicate and to give meaning to our reality. Effective language use can be difficult to achieve. According to the linguist Erica Huls, people use language strategically in order to project an image of themselves in the eyes of others:

According to politeness theory, people make strategic choices in their interaction with others. For example, they can be direct or indirect, attentive or give each other space, they can cut straight to the chase or keep their cards close to their chest. However, this does not mean that people are sophisticated and calculating strategists who constantly and meticulously control their every word.

(Huls, 2002)

Here, the term 'strategy' implies that to at least a small degree, people reflect upon how they formulate their communication. Communication is more than just sharing information – the way we communicate shapes our interpersonal relationships. Communication lays the foundations upon which social relationships are built.

An adapted form of *politeness theory*, which is illustrated by the above quote, lies at the very heart of the eCP method. This theory was developed in the 1970s by the two linguists Penelope Brown and Stephen Levinson and then extensively researched within a wide range of cultures and circumstances. In order to create the eCP method, the work of Brown and Levinson, in addition to the work of Huls, was translated and applied into a coaching context, with particular focus on the coach–client relationship. The goal of politeness theory is to explain universal commonalities occurring within the linguistic patterns that people use when showing consideration for each other. Politeness theory focuses on language and interaction. In principle, the theory relates to all interpersonal activities with any linguistic basis. The main question of politeness theory is 'How do people show consideration for each other when communicating?' This not only relates to how you show people respect or give people space, but also how you make it clear that you like each other. Examples of linguistic devices include explanations, questions, flattery, obscenities, compliments, criticism, promises, greetings, congratulations etc. These devices are known as speech acts.

Our brain works hard every time we express ourselves, whether we are saying something original or repeating familiar patterns. Fundamentally, the formulation of sentences is not an automatic process, as people know that there are many different ways to express things. In general, we have very little time to weigh-up the possibilities and we respond semi-automatically. This is particularly the case in F2F conversations. Within e-coaching programmes that include no F2F contact and use only written communication to build-up social and interpersonal relationships, you have plenty of time to make deliberate, strategic and efficient decisions regarding the language you use. You have plenty of time to decide which speech acts to use and why. In the following sections, we will further explain the application of politeness theory.

6.3 An arsenal of linguistic strategies

Politeness theory explains how people show consideration for each other. The concept of saving face is a central aspect of politeness theory. Saving face is a vital factor during interpersonal interaction. Politeness theory asserts that saving face is a basic human need that involves two key factors. On the one hand, people need to feel like they have their own space (independence), and they therefore maintain sufficient distance from others. On the other hand, humans cannot develop in total isolation (dependence). As a result, humans require appreciation and approval from others, but also need to be an independent person whose actions are unimpeded by other people. By using speech acts (any human interaction involving language), we run the risk of infringing upon our interlocutor's need to save face. Choosing from the various speech acts during social interaction is a continual process of balancing the need to save face for yourself and the need to save face for the person you are talking to. The dilemma in this process is to avoid lapsing into intrusiveness on the one hand and aloofness on the other. This dilemma is illustrated by the following example: Imagine you wish to give someone constructive criticism. In effect, this is infringing on somebody's personal space, as you are giving unsolicited feedback about somebody else's behaviour. In order to cushion the effect of this intrusion, you could combine the feedback with a compliment. The deliberate use of this speech act softens your message and shows that you care about the other person's basic need to feel valued and respected and that it is important to you to maintain a relationship with this person.

The need to save face is the primary basis for the various linguistic strategies identified by Brown and Levinson. In total, there are forty different linguistic strategies divided into five main categories that reflect how direct or indirect they are. Here, the word 'direct' means that the chosen linguistic strategy is formulated in a way that can have only one meaning or interpretation. An indirect linguistic strategy is formulated in such a way that it can be interpreted in a number of ways. The speaker therefore cannot be pinned down to a single meaning. Another way in which the categories can be classified is on a scale ranging from 'gets close to the other person' to 'maintains distance from the other person'. In this respect, direct communication is extremely effective in getting close to the other person and indirect communication is effective at keeping your distance. The linguistic strategies are divided into the following categories:

1 Direct with positive language means focused on the relationship.
2 Direct without positive language means.
3 Indirect.
4 Indirect positive language means focused on the relationship.
5 Don't perform the speech act.

The choice of linguistic strategy is a delicate question. If you are too direct, you could be seen as being blunt. If you are too indirect, you run the risk of being unclear and inefficient, which can cause misunderstandings. If you are too respectful, you could be seen as being too stiff. If you are too jovial, you risk overstepping boundaries. According to politeness theory, there are also three situational factors that influence the correct choice of linguistic strategy:

1 Balance of power.
2 Social distance.
3 Intrusiveness of the speech act.

Within coaching relationships, there is usually no balance of power. The relationship and the interaction between the two are always conducted carefully, respectfully and on a basis of equality. The second factor – social distance – is usually greater at the start of a coaching programme, as the coach and client don't know each other yet. The less familiar with each other the two parties are, the more linguistic devices are required in order to bridge the gap. Combining direct messages with extra words that cushion the message does this. For example:

> Via e-mail, I could ask my new client 'Tell me something about yourself'. This is a very direct formulation of a simple question, and to somebody you hardly know, it could sound blunt. It is therefore useful to phrase it differently, such as 'Would you like to tell me about yourself?' In this way, I get a better impression of you, which in turn helps me to do my job.

The less social distance, the more direct you can be in your use of language. The third factor is the intrusiveness of the speech act. Essentially, all speech acts intrude on people's personal space to a certain degree, although some more than others. When sensitive issues are the subject of discussion, greater caution is advised as the subject in itself is emotionally charged. Strategic, clear and carefully phrased language is therefore essential in such situations.

6.4 Politeness theory for e-coaching: three relevant language strategies

In e-mail coaching, there is only a limited amount of non-verbal communication. As a result, the risk of misunderstandings is increased and important signals are omitted. Every type of misinterpretation must be prevented, which requires very careful language use by the coach. Due to this risk, the coach must avoid using indirect linguistic strategies. Indirect formulations can confuse the client, which must be avoided at all costs during written forms of e-coaching. Of the categories of linguistic strategies used in e-coaching (see Section 6.3), it is the direct strategies that the coach must use in order to get closer to the client and establish optimal co-operation. The three groups of linguistic strategies that can be used within the eCP method are:

1 Direct positive language means focused on the relationship.
2 Direct without positive language means.
3 Don't perform the speech act.

Below is an explanation of these three relevant groups of linguistic strategies.

6.4.1 Group 1: Direct positive language means focused on the relationship

This is the most complex of the strategy groups listed in Section 6.3, due to the usage of various kinds of positive language means focused on the relationship. These strategies are frequently used within professional relationships and are ideal for e-mail coaching. The structural use of positive language means focused on the relationship involves specific linguistic strategies, i.e. strategies to build closer connections. These are crucial at the beginning of the coaching process, and we will therefore explain them first.

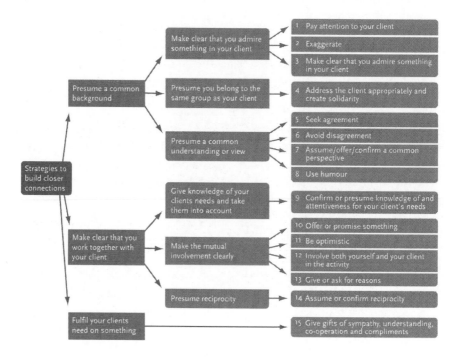

FIGURE 6.1 Overview of strategies to build closer connections

Source: Ribbers and Waringa (2012) based on Huls (2001)

When employing strategies to build closer connections, the process of formulating direct messages is facilitated by positive language means focused on the relationship. The purpose of strategies to build closer connections is to allow the sender (the coach) to project a positive image of him/herself in the mind of the receiver (the client) by showing that they are sensitive of the receiver's needs (in this case, the need to save face). There are fifteen different strategies to build closer connections that can be used in accordance with the situation and the client's needs. For each main strategy, there are a number of subcategories, each of which differs with regard to the degree of *social acceleration*. This acceleration shows how much closer the coach–client relationship has become. The first sub strategy contributes most to the degree of closeness, and the last sub strategy contributes the least. All of the sub strategies serve to reduce the social distance between coach and client. Figure. 6.1 displays an overview of the available strategies to build closer connections. The fifteen strategies to build closer connections can be applied in written communication at the coach's own discretion. They are most literally applied when formulating an e-mail. When writing a response to a client's question, the first step is to establish an objective: what does the coach want to achieve with this message, and what elements must be included in the e-mail in order to do this? Consider the following example:

> You receive an e-mail from a client. Based on your interpretation and analysis, you conclude that the client has a need for affirmation or a stimulus because you noticed that the client is doubtful about a certain subject. The best strategy in this case is therefore 'satisfy your client's need for something'. You could satisfy this need by displaying understanding for their feelings, by positively reinforcing the effort they have made or by emphasizing the achievements that they have made. You then round it off with a compliment. Subsequently, you can show your involvement (use main strategy 2, subcategory 2) by expressing optimism about the next steps that the client is going to take.

This is a simple example of how the strategies can be applied. In spoken communication, you don't have enough time to consider in detail which linguistic strategy you should use and when. In their everyday practice, experienced coaches will already use many of the previously mentioned strategies without even realizing it. However, the asynchronicity of e-mail coaching enables you to consciously examine your use of language strategies, which enables the coaching process to be designed and structured more effectively.

6.4.2 Group 2: Direct without positive language means

The Direct without positive language means strategy is used in relationships between people who know each other, are close, have a bond of trust and feel free to communicate directly. Within a coaching programme, this linguistic strategy will at first be used to a lesser degree as the relationship is still developing and the boundaries are still being laid. The further the programme progresses and the stronger the relationship becomes, the more direct you can make the communication. Directness can help make the communication more personal. As a result, this strategy helps reduce inhibition and increases participation, openness and honesty, which makes it a hugely important strategy for e-coaching. The better the coach and client get to know each other during the coaching programme, and hence the lesser the social distance between them becomes, the more direct language can be used without positive language means (i.e. positive language means focused on the relationship).

6.4.3 Group 3: Don't perform the speech act

The asynchronicity of the communication and the written messages used to conduct it means that you don't have to respond immediately and you have more time to think about and reflect upon your answer. Furthermore, another possibility is available that can sometimes cause awkwardness in F2F coaching: deliberately not responding to something the client says. After all, it is not always necessary to respond to everything. An e-mail coach has to make many more choices about which statements or issues to address – and why – than his F2F counterparts. You must also be equally careful when choosing what not to address. For these reasons, this strategy is very frequently used in e-mail coaching.

6.5 Linguistic analysis and speech acts

To maximize the efficiency of the dialogue, the coach must select the best linguistic strategy and determine how it can be most effectively employed. To do this, begin by analysing the client's messages. The eCP method uses linguistic analysis based on speech acts in order to structurally analyse clients' messages. The linguist John Searle grouped all speech acts into five main categories:

1. Assertives
These are speech acts that the speaker uses to say something about the reality of both the speaker and the hearer. When using an assertive, you attempt to convince the recipient of the message that they also believe in the truth of the assertive. Examples of these include assertions (compliments and criticisms), descriptions, explanations, conclusions, observations and assumptions.

2. Directives
These are attempts to influence the behaviour of the person you are addressing. The intention is that the hearer displays the behaviour requested or desired by the speaker. Examples include requests, questions, warnings and advice.

3. Expressives
These sincerely communicate the inner feelings, attitudes and emotions of the speaker. Examples include gratitude, congratulations, sorrow, greetings, apologies and welcomes.

4. Commissives
Speech acts in this category relate to promises, vows and guarantees. They indicate

that an obligation has been created. Examples include promises, oaths, agreements, assurances and threats.

5. Declaratives
These speech acts communicate a change in reality pursuant to the proposal of the declaration. In other words, they signify a change in status or condition effective as of the moment the declaration is made. Examples of such statements include 'The meeting is now in session', 'You're fired', 'I quit' or 'I now pronounce you husband and wife'.

By classifying every sentence of your e-mail in accordance with the above groups, you can systematically assess which speech acts have been used. For example, if a client uses a large number of expressives, the coach can conclude that the client requires recognition of their emotions. The coach's response is also made up of multiple speech acts, so these messages can also be analysed and monitored before being sent to the client in order to complete the communication cycle. In Part II of the book, we will further elaborate on how coaches can use linguistic analysis to more objectively evaluate what their clients are trying to say and how they can optimally formulate their own messages to the client.

6.6 Efficient use of language

One of the core principles of the eCP method is effective, targeted language. In effect, the speakers co-operate within a dialogue, and for this reason, eCP dialogues are conducted in accordance with the cooperative principle. The language philosopher Paul Grice, who meticulously studied the basic conditions for efficient language usage, formulated it. He defined four simple principles known as the *Gricean Maxims*, that form the basis of efficient language use and therefore enable optimum co-operation between coach and client. These maxims can be used to make the communication more functional and effective. The four Gricean Maxims are:

1   *Relation:* Is what you have said relevant?
2   *Quantity:* Is what you have said sufficiently but not excessively informative?
3   *Quality:* Is the content and structure of what you have said of sufficient quality?
4   *Clearness:* Is what you have said clear, unambiguous and understandable?

By applying these maxims, the coach can filter out irrelevant words, unclear wordings, improbabilities and exaggerations from their messages. Whenever these maxims are not applied, there is a greater likelihood that interpretation mechanisms will come into play, resulting in the recipient interpreting something other than the literal meaning. By properly applying the maxims when writing messages, you can eliminate misinterpretations. For this reason, coaches using the eCP method must apply these four maxims to write and scrutinize every message they write.

6.7 Summary

In this chapter, we examined the opportunities for making strategic usage of language within e-mail coaching. The asynchronous nature of e-mail communication means that the coach has plenty of time to analyse every message received and to determine the correct strategies to use. The coach can use this knowledge to make sure the coaching process runs smoothly. The eCoachPro method gives you a structured method for realizing a productive professional relationship. The method was developed using aspects of 'politeness theory', which focuses on how people mould their interpersonal relationships using language. Various strategies can be used depending on the type of relationship, what stage the relationship is at, and the social distance between the parties involved. Three strategies can be used within the eCP method: 1) Direct positive language means focused on the relationship, 2) Direct without positive language means or 3) don't perform the speech act.

A frequently used strategy is to be direct in combination with positive language means focused on the relationship. In this way, the coach tries to get closer to the client and project a positive image of him/herself in the client's mind by showing that they are considerate of the client's needs (i.e. their need to save face). This encourages the client to actively participate in the coaching process. In order to analyse the client's messages, the eCP method makes use of speech-act analysis. Speech acts are all language-related devices that we use in our interpersonal contact with others. These speech acts are divided into five main categories: Assertives, which state something about reality; Directives, which attempt to influence the behaviour of others; Expressives, which communicate the feelings, attitudes or emotions of the speaker; Commissives, which indicate the establishment of an obligation; and Declaratives, which categorically proclaim that a particular status has been assigned. Based on the speech acts used in a client's message, the coach can determine the appropriate linguistic strategy to use in order to optimize their response. Once the coach has formulated their response, the Gricean Maxims for effective language use can be employed to check the coach's message with regard to relation, quantity, quality and clearness. The speech acts, linguistic strategies and the Gricean Maxims are all integral parts of the eCP method. In Part II of this book, we will illustrate how the eCP method can be applied in practice and the entire technical context of e-coaching will be explained.

PART II

Working as an e-coach

In Part I of this book, we discussed a variety of the aspects, theories and background information relating to e-coaching, such as the different types of e-coaching (in particular e-mail coaching). We established that e-coaching is a special type of coaching that differs from traditional face-to-face (F2F) coaching in relation to a number of key aspects. In practice, it has been shown that when getting started, many coaches have difficulty getting to grips with the e-coaching process. In order to conduct an effective coaching program online, you must master the specific processes and the dynamics created by online communication. To give coaches greater insight into the e-coaching process, we have developed the Accelerated Behavioural Change (ABC) model, together with the special eCoachPro (eCP) method.

In Part I, we provided a description of this model and method and explained its theoretical foundations. In Part II, we will show you how to practically integrate the ABC model and the eCP method into your professional e-coaching practice. However, before we do this, we will give the results of a study we carried out amongst a group of experienced e-coaches. The practical application of the model and the step-by-step plan behind the method are based on the real-life professional experiences of these e-coaches. In e-coaching, the use of information and communication technology (ICT) plays an essential role, and the use of computers, the Internet, smartphones etc. gives the e-coaching process a unique constitution and dynamics.

We will conclude this part of the book with a summary of all preconditions necessary to conduct a successful e-coaching programme.

7

EXPERIENCES OF E-COACHES

More and more coaches are choosing to expand their coaching arsenal to include e-coaching. For many years, a large proportion of traditional F2F coaches have supplemented their practice with telephone calls, Skype calls and the occasional e-mail. In the previous chapters, we have shown that getting started with e-coaching involves a great deal of change for coaches, requiring them to learn new skills and overcome a number of challenges such as the lack of non-verbal communication. In order to gain insight into the changing role of the coach and what e-coaching means to coaches, we surveyed a number of e-coaches about their experiences.

To do this, we devised a brief questionnaire and shared it amongst a group of coaches who have worked with e-coaching. We primarily focused on coaches who have worked with e-mail coaching, as this type of e-coaching is the most distinct from traditional F2F coaching. The questionnaire consisted of a number of open questions and was completed by 37 coaches.[1] All of them are certified by professional organizations like the International Coaching Federation (ICF), European Mentoring and Coaching Council (EMCC) or the Association for Coaching (AC). Between them, they possess 332 years of coaching experience and have conducted 334 e-coaching programs.

NB: As we are displaying the answers to open questions, we sometimes make use of percentages. For example, if 10 coaches give a similar answer, we state that 27 per cent of the coaches expressed this opinion. However, this percentage does not necessarily mean that 73 per cent of the coaches did not share this opinion, just that they didn't specifically state it. In this chapter, the results of the questionnaire will be summarized in a number of themed sections.

Spotlight 1: Less is more

Coaching objective: Learn to be more flexible when dealing with employees. Client is female. Contact frequency: twice a week. Program length: three weeks.

The fewer questions I asked, the more I motivated my client to act. Upon my shortest question – 'What would you like to do with this insight? – she really sprang into action.

Coach: Judith Groenendijk

7.1 Reasons for getting started with e-coaching

A majority of the coaches (55 per cent) said they believe e-coaching is the future of coaching and that it helps them adapt to modern developments (Internet communication, increasing use of social media etc.) A third of the coaches stated that e-coaching will provide new opportunities and target groups, especially as it serves as an excellent supplement to F2F coaching. The coaches also recognize that it offers certain advantages over F2F coaching. In addition to the fact that you can provide more intensive coaching, 30 per cent of the coaches mentioned the greater flexibility provided by the time and location independence. A few specifically state that e-coaching makes it easier to balance their work and personal lives. Some coaches say that they have an affinity for the written word and recognize the value that writing adds to the coaching process. Two coaches said that initially, they were resistant to the change and had little faith in it, which was a significant obstacle to them moving into e-coaching. However, once they got started with it, their enthusiasm grew rapidly. Just one of the coaches says that he has since stopped offering e-coaching as it offered less than he had expected.

7.2 Important similarities and differences between e-coaching and F2F coaching

The similarities reported by the coaches can generally be divided into four categories: objectives, relationship, structure and techniques. A significant majority (65 per cent) of the coaches stated that in both types of coaching, the coach works in a goal- and result-orientated manner. With guidance from the coach, the client determines the points for improvement. Also, 19 per cent find that certain subgoals and secondary objectives greatly match the content of the coaching, such as improving the client's reflection skills, increasing self-awareness and changing behaviour in practice. A third of the coaches emphasized that with both types of coaching, it is important to create a safe environment for the client and develop a bond of trust. A number of coaches also think that both types of coaching offer a

---

Spotlight 2: Enabling immediate intervention

Coaching objective: To develop self-confidence and be less emotional when making decisions. Combination of F2F and e-mail coaching (20 weeks). Contact frequency varied depending on how the client was feeling each week.

The client works as an account manager and always receives high evaluation results. This year, he was evaluated by his mentor rather than his manager. However, he has been in conflict with his mentor for months, and his score for various aspects dropped significantly without any reasons being given. The evaluation was sent in writing and had to be signed immediately. The client was upset and angry and e-mailed me on Friday afternoon. He mentioned a variety of responses that he wanted to give, most of them governed by emotion. The only reaction I gave by e-mail was 'Do you want to be happy or do you want to be right?' He said later that this immediate intervention helped him to avoid ruining his weekend by obsessing about the situation. He then settled this dispute calmly, professionally and to his satisfaction the following week.

Coach: Yvonne Breur-Huisman

---

systematic structure to the process, enabling many useful methods and techniques to be applied. Nearly half stated that the techniques used in F2F coaching were entirely suitable for e-coaching. Examples given include asking questions, listening (which equates to careful reading when applied to e-mail coaching), persisting with difficult questions and giving positive reinforcement in order to boost motivation.

According to 85 per cent of the coaches, the main difference between e-coaching and F2F coaching is the communication method used. This not only relates to the use of the written word instead of speech, but also the fact that e-coaching is both time and location independent, which enables flexible frequency of communication. In addition to the communication methods, many other practical benefits of e-coaching were mentioned, such as the lack of travelling time/costs and not having to rent office space.

Two coaches experienced in the field of provocative coaching indicated that e-coaching is less suitable for being confrontational with the client, as this can come across differently in writing. A few coaches believe that e-coaching can't be compared to F2F coaching because of the lack of non-verbal communication.

Spotlight 3: The five-minute breakthrough

Coaching objective: Relieve work-related stress. Female client, combination of F2F coaching and e-coaching. Contact frequency: one session per week, later one session every two or three weeks. Duration: twelve weeks.

The end of the coaching programme was in sight, with the end date after Christmas. The client had had a major setback. Because I didn't want to abandon her over the Christmas period and given how serious her setback had been, we agreed to chat once a week via WhatsApp. This made sure that she wouldn't feel alone and would help to boost her confidence. In the end, we only needed to chat for a very short time before she recovered her focus and balanced her mood. Just five minutes on WhatsApp was all she needed – now that's what I call a success!

Coach: Judith Den Haan

7.3 Important advantages and disadvantages of e-coaching

Forty-three per cent of the coaches had difficulty with the fact that they and their clients were not simultaneously present. The lack of non-verbal communication was stated as the main reason for this difficulty. Other reasons given were that it is more difficult to assess the client's emotional state and that it is harder to check whether the client has properly received and understood the information or intended meaning. It is also difficult to explain things as you can't physically demonstrate to them. The main advantage reported was that because the two parties couldn't see each other, the client felt less inhibited and was able to get to the point quicker. A third of the coaches mentioned that due to the asynchronous nature of the communication, you can give more thought to your responses and edit them as often as you wish before sending. A number of coaches say they find it useful that the client can reread the messages as many times as they want.

Forty per cent of the coaches state that the opportunity for more frequent and intensive contact with the client is the main reason for the effectiveness of e-coaching. A few of the coaches have already experienced for themselves how the greater intensity of e-coaching and the smaller steps it enables results in quicker progress than with F2F programmes.

Finally, it was mentioned that payment is riskier with e-coaching, as part or all of the payment is due after completion of the course, but you have often never met the client in person.

Spotlight 4: The surplus of written reflections

Coaching objective: how can I, being an introvert man, manage and influence my international team of smart professionals? Male client, head R&D global organization. Combination of F2F coaching and e-coaching. Contact frequency: one F2F session per month plus e-mail contact twice a week. Duration: four months.

In the beginning, the client had the strong belief that introvert people are not able to influence others because of their attitude of waiting. After he could make a shift in this irrational belief he practiced different behaviour and eagerly wrote down his well-considered reflections on these experiments. Because of the regular frequency of sharing his written reflections with the coach, his self-confidence improved. He had the courage to rely on his intuition and he developed a natural way of influencing, regardless of being introvert or extravert. During the evaluation he pointed out that in particular the sharing of his written reflections with his coach had accelerated his internalization process and has contributed to a higher self-esteem and more powerful approach to others.

Coach: Margreet Steenbrink

7.4 What skills do e-coaches need?

Sixty-five per cent of the coaches stated that the most important skill for e-coaches is the ability to write concisely. Half of the coaches say that the communication method forces them to use language in a different way compared to F2F coaching sessions. For example, the language use is more goal-oriented and less focused on interpretation, i.e. fewer assumptions are made and you only respond to what is literally written down.

Another important skill mentioned is the ability to ration your questions. In e-mail coaching, you must limit the number of questions you pose, so the ones you do ask have to be effective and comprehensive. A striking skill mentioned is the need to have more 'patience' when formulating messages.

Time-management skills are also noted, although not always in the same way. Some of the coaches find it difficult to schedule enough time for e-coaching or to respond to the client's messages on time. However, others have the opposite problem, stating that they spend too much time on their e-coaching programmes. They get sucked into the coaching process, which can blur the line between their work and personal lives.

Just 10 per cent of the coaches stated that being good with ICT equipment (computers, the Internet, e-mail programs etc.) is a precondition for being an effective e-coach.

A noticeable factor was the large number of comments about the coaches' own doubts. Reasons for these doubts included worrying if their message conveyed the right tone of voice, wondering whether e-coaching is suitable for certain clients, uncertainty about clients' reluctance, uncertainty about responsibility for coaching progress and working too hard to keep the client involved. More tools and insight into e-coaching could help reduce this level of uncertainty for coaches. One coach stated that the reason for these doubts could simply be caused by lack of experience.

Finally, being able to encourage the client online is mentioned as an important skill to help prevent the coaching process from stagnating.

Spotlight 5: Rapid results despite having doubts

Career coaching: taking the next step in your career. Client is female. Contact frequency: three sessions per week. Duration: three weeks.

The client answers all of my questions quickly and effectively and carries out the assignments competently. However, she never uses greetings or sign-offs in her messages, which came over as being quite blunt. After a week, I started to worry that I was doing something wrong. However, in her next e-mail she suddenly started to use them, and also wrote about how she likes this form of communication and enjoys carrying out the assignments. From this, I learned that I should have confidence that I'm doing things right. I also noticed that the extremely frequent contact enabled the client to make a lot of progress in just a week and a half. Working together in such an intensive and targeted manner enables you to get to the heart of the matter very quickly.

Coach: Rita Vanelderen

7.5 Tips for both beginner and experienced e-coaches

The coaches surveyed also gave a number of tips for other e-coaches and professionals who are about to take their first steps into the world of e-coaching. The tips can be divided into two categories: e-coaching tips and business tips.

Tips to ensure successful e-coaching programmes:

- Adjust your communication style to suit the medium you are using.
- Prevent misunderstandings by formulating clear and concise messages.
- Invest in developing a good professional relationship, e.g. by giving lots of compliments.
- Ensure that you continually motivate your client.

- Set assignments that get clients to examine themselves and their behaviour.
- Extensive responses are not necessary.
- Try not to address every single point in the client's message in detail.
- Avoid prejudgment, assumptions and interpretations: read only the lines instead of trying to read between them as well.
- Check your messages thoroughly to ensure your spelling and grammar is correct.
- Look for positive achievements in the client's messages and emphasize them.

Spotlight 6: Strategic language use

Coaching objective: Paying attention to the person behind the employee. Client is a manager in the healthcare sector. Coaching frequency: two sessions per week. Duration: twelve weeks.

In F2F coaching, I am not afraid to confront clients or to say things that 'shouldn't' be said. However, I have learned that it is harder to do this with e-coaching and that you have to use a more strategic approach. During a particular coaching programme, I read between the lines that the client doesn't really pay attention to others, and phrased my response as follows: 'From what you have said, it looks like you only seek contact if there is a functional reason to do so. It seems that your conversations always have a goal and that making contact with others is not a goal in itself. Does this sound right? Don't be afraid to say if I'm mistaken, as with email coaching, everything is in writing and it's difficult to check whether I'm on the right track.' He wrote back that I'd 'hit the nail on the head', confirming that my suspicion was correct. With this knowledge, I was able to set the following self-awareness exercise:

Take a notepad and make two sections: 'Interested' and other 'Not Interested'. Add one to the 'Not Interested' tally if you notice that you are not really interested in making contact with the other person in a conversation, and add one to the 'Interested' tally if you are.

Result: The client's self-awareness has increased and he opened up more to his employees. The best evidence of his success in this area was that during the coaching programme, his employees started to open up to him about problems they were having (both work-related and personal) without him asking. Before the coaching programme, they never would have done this.

Coach: Annette Lechner

Business tips:

- Carefully consider whether e-coaching suits you (an affinity for language seems to be an important aspect).
- Integrate e-coaching into the services you provide.
- Be aware that in the initial stages, you will have to invest a great deal of time in order to master e-coaching.
- Carefully select a specific type of e-coaching and ICT equipment.
- Get an experienced e-coach to supervise you while starting up your e-coaching practice.
- Invest in training.
- Practice with test clients or fellow coaches.
- Build up your confidence in e-coaching.
- Take time to convince clients of the power of e-coaching and the opportunities it provides.
- Ensure effective time management. If you're not careful, you could end up working 24/7!

Spotlight 7: Allowing the client to set the pace

Coaching objective: What do I need to do to shape a divided team into one? Client is male and works as a manager. Contact frequency: three times a week. Duration: ten weeks.

A striking moment in this coaching programme was something that happened after a few weeks: so far, the client was taking very small steps. However, all of a sudden, I found a detailed plan for a team-building afternoon in his online exercise book! This showed that he had taken the new insights to heart and was able to apply them in practice. I learned that I may be confident that my clients choose their own natural pace, even if I think they could go faster. The team-building afternoon turned out to be a great success!

Coach: Viola Majoie

7.6 Hybrid coaching: combining F2F coaching with e-coaching

Two thirds of the coaches indicated that after their experiences with e-coaching, they adjusted how they work as an F2F coach. They stated that they are more conscious of their language use, they pay more attention to what they say and that the quality of the questions they ask has improved. They also ask fewer questions.

A third of these coaches said that they now give more compliments during their F2F sessions (e-coaching made them realize how infrequently they did this beforehand). Twenty-seven per cent of these coaches have incorporated exercises from e-coaching into their F2F programmes. Nearly all coaches said that they would use e-coaching techniques to support them in their F2F coaching. A small percentage of these coaches even believed that combining these two types of coaching makes it possible to achieve the coaching objectives sooner.

Spotlight 8: Ideal combination of F2F and e-coaching

Coaching objective: Examining own motives and recognizing own limitations. Client is male and works for a mail-order company. Contact frequency: one F2F session per month plus weekly e-mail contact. Duration: five months.

At work, the client finds that he has difficulty setting boundaries for himself and his co-workers. The underlying issue to this is that he doesn't know what motivates him and what he really wants.

An in-depth session once a month helps him to work on his verbal and non-verbal communication when setting boundaries. The assignments that he is set during the coaching programme can be immediately applied at work. He also uses an online exercise book to note down moments of success and any challenges he encounters. Being able to use the exercise book to get things off his chest if and when he needs to is very helpful to him. He particularly finds that writing about things that go wrong helps him to develop his self-reflection skills.

Coach: Charlotte van den Wall Bake

7.7 Summary

In this chapter, we summarized what e-coaches have to say about their practical e-coaching experiences. We did this by creating a survey featuring a number of open questions. The questionnaire was completed by 37 coaches who have completed 334 e-coaching programs between them. The results of the survey were divided into a number of themes. The majority of the coaches believe that e-coaching is the future. In addition, a majority sees great similarities between F2F and e-coaching. The main difference between the two types is in the manner of communication. A proportion of the coaches stated that the nature of e-mail communication (asynchronous, remote, written) enables more frequent and intensive contact with the client. Less than half of the coaches consider e-coaching's lack of non-verbal communication to be a problem. The coaches indicated that in order to conduct effective e-coaching, you must be concise in your communication, ration your questions, resist the temptation to make your own interpretations of what the client is saying, and manage your time effectively and efficiently. They also offered a list of tips for coaches who are getting started with e-coaching. These tips included building a good professional relationship with your client by giving lots of compliments, carefully avoiding spelling mistakes and bad grammar, writing concise messages, investing in training, and getting plenty of practice before offering e-coaching as a professional service. Finally, it turned out that most of these coaches have incorporated e-coaching into their F2F programmes.

Both the positive and negative experiences with e-coaching can be easily explained by the characteristics of this type of coaching as described in Part I. The application of the ABC model and the eCP method within e-coaching programmes enables more frequent sharing and reinforcement of positive experiences. In the next two chapters, we show how this model and method can be successfully applied in practice.

Note

1   The group consists of 27 women and 10 men with an average age of 46.6 years.

8
THE ABC MODEL IN PRACTICE

In this chapter, we will show you how to apply the Accelerated Behavioural Change model in practice in order to design and execute e-coaching programmes. As the emphasis in this chapter is on the practical integration of the model, we will only make limited reference to the theory behind the model. For more detailed information about the theoretical basis of the model, see Chapter 5.

In this chapter, we will illustrate the various steps in the ABC model by means of a simple example (see Figure 8.1). The example relates to a manager of a

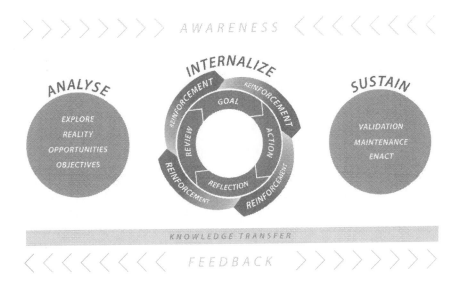

FIGURE 8.1 The ABC model
Source: © Ribbers and Waringa (2011)

financial organization who wants to undergo a coaching programme. The objective of this programme is to 'learn to give better feedback'. Giving feedback is one of the most valuable activities in the workplace, although people find it very difficult to get it right. In this example, the goal is to learn a new kind of behaviour, and we will achieve it by means of the three stages of the ABC model.

8.1 A practical example of the ABC model

8.1.1 Phase 1: Analyse

In this stage, the client (a manager) and the coach explore the true nature of the coaching objective. This will be done by means of the following four steps: *Explore – Reality – Opportunities – Objectives*.

Phase 1: Analyse

1   *Explore:* This is the fact-finding stage conducted at the beginning of every coaching programme. Here, the manager and the coach will get to know each other and to take the first steps in the coaching relationship. The coach will also investigate the exact reasons behind the manager's decision to get coaching and establish the issues relating to the coaching objective. The manager's objective for the coaching is to learn to give better feedback, so questions that the coach could ask include:
   •   How would you define feedback?
   •   What does feedback mean to you?
   •   Is feedback important to you?
   •   On a scale of 1 to 10, how good would you say you are at giving feedback?

2   *Reality:* Next, it is important that the coach examines and maps out the manager's current behaviour regarding feedback. Possible questions that the coach can ask in this step include:
   •   How often do you give feedback?
   •   How do you give feedback?
   •   What are your strong and weak points when giving feedback?
   •   Do the recipients of your feedback take it the right way?
   •   If you asked a colleague/friend/family member to describe how you give feedback, what would they say?

In addition, the coach may ask the manager to write down a practical example, describing in detail how he gave feedback in a particular situation and how the recipient responded to it.

3   *Opportunities:* Using the insights gained in the previous step, the coach will examine the options open to the manager. In this context, the term 'opportunities' refers to realistic and desirable future situations. The coach will examine the manager's current situation and assess how it can contribute to realizing the coaching objective. Questions that the coach may ask in this step of the process include:
   - What do you want to change about the way you give feedback?
   - What would be noticeably different if you made this change?
   - How do you want people to respond to your feedback?
   - What do you need in order to give better feedback? (e.g. knowledge, skills, support, money, time)
   - What steps have you already taken to improve your feedback?
   - What are suitable moments to work on your feedback skills?
   - What are the possible obstacles to giving better feedback and how could you remove them or get round them?

4   *Objectives:* Once the exploratory phase is complete, it will be completely clear what the manager wants to achieve and what he will need to do so. With this information, you can set the definitive coaching objective. This objective can consist of one or more subgoals. Once this main objective has been set, the manager formulates it in greater detail, such as:

'I want to learn how to give regular feedback as effectively as possible regarding the performance and behaviour of my employees in a way that will be positively received.'

8.1.2 Phase 2: Internalize

Phase 2: Internalize

In stage 2, the manager will actively work towards achieving the objective as defined in stage 1, under the supervision of the coach.

A key factor in this stage is positive *reinforcement*. Within the working environment, the manager will actively perform the exercises assigned by the coach. Practicing with new behaviour when interacting with colleagues will result in positive reactions. These positive reactions (reinforcement) to the manager's new behaviour help to embed it in his nature, as the positive response that it gains from his environment encourages him to display the behaviour more often. The manager's experiences will also be shared with the coach, who will provide further positive reinforcement of the manager's new behaviour. As a result, the manager will receive acknowledgement from multiple sources, which will help accelerate the internalization process for this new behaviour.

The model operates on the premise that small steps result in the greatest levels of success and facilitate behavioural change. For this reason, stage 2 begins by splitting the coaching objective into subgoals.

1   *Goal:* The first step for the manager is to define a subgoal in operational terms, e.g. 'This week, I want to practice giving feedback using the tips given by my coach.' This is a good opportunity for the coach to provide information about feedback (*knowledge transfer*). For example, plenty of useful information is available about how to use feedback as an instrument and you can also find tips and rules that can help optimize feedback. This information gives the manager extra support in his voyage of discovery. With a clear objective and useful information in mind, the manager can work towards achieving his first subgoal.

2   *Action:* The second step is all about converting words into action. Exercises and assignments are central to the process, and the manager will carry them out in his workplace. An example of an assignment could be 'this week, you will schedule a one-on-one meeting with an employee and give them feedback.' This is a concrete and straightforward assignment that requires the manager to take action. He will directly experience the effect of the new behaviour, both internally and on his environment (in this case the recipient of the feedback). In order to make the learning experience stick, the next step is of critical importance.

3   *Reflection:* In the third step, the coach will help the manager to reflect upon the exercise and ask him about the emotions, thoughts and feelings he experienced during the exercise. The following is an example of this kind of reflection by the manager: 'I prepared well for the meeting. I gave feedback during a one-on-one meeting and I was quite nervous beforehand. It felt good, I followed the recommended instructions and the feedback was positively received.' (This is a brief summary: in practice, the reflection must be much more extensive.) Reflecting on the experience in this way helps the manager to process the experience both cognitively and emotionally.

4   *Review:* In Step four, all of the previous steps will be evaluated. The coach will ask the manager to list everything that he has learned during the assignment. The coach and client will also determine whether the goal has been sufficiently realized. The coach could use any of the following questions:
    • How do you feel about giving feedback now?
    • How often do you apply the things you have learned?
    • How do your employees receive the new behaviour?
    • Give an example of how you give feedback now.

- Are you satisfied with the way you give feedback?
- On a scale from 1 to 10, how would you rate your current feedback skills?

If the exercise has helped the manager to sufficiently achieve his subgoal, then he can formulate a new subgoal. The manager could also decide that the exercise was not relevant enough to the subgoal and/or that he needs more practice before he can say he has realized the desired situation. In this event, the coach can decide to adjust or repeat the assignment. The coach could also decide to increase the difficulty level of the assignment and take things one step further. The following is an example of a manager's evaluation: 'The exercise went well, but I think I'd like to practice it again a couple of times to make sure I've got the knack. Next week, for example, I'd like to give three people feedback about their performance.' This shows that he has taken the time to analyse his situation and modified his subgoal to give him more practice.

During the internalization stage, it can occur that the four-step plan is repeated several times before the client is satisfied with the results achieved. In accordance with the 'baby steps' principle, the smaller the subgoal, the greater the chances of success. This increased number of successes helps reinforce and motivate the client, which accelerates the process of behavioural change. This principle is reflected in Figure 8.2.

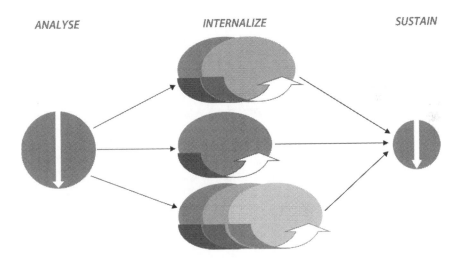

ANALYSE   *INTERNALIZE*   *SUSTAIN*

FIGURE 8.2 Execution of the ABC model

The transition from stage 2 to stage 3 only takes place once the subgoals have been achieved, i.e. for each subgoal in the evaluation, the manager has achieved sufficient behavioural change and the new behaviour now feels natural.

8.1.3 Phase 3: Sustain

In this stage, you will determine whether the goals set in stage 1 have been truly achieved and identify what the manager may still need in order to maintain the newly learned behaviour. If internalization has truly taken place and the new behaviour is firmly embedded in the manager's cognitive processes, then stage 3 will take very little time.

Phase 3: Sustain

1   *Validation:* The first step focuses on whether the predefined goals have been achieved in the eyes of the manager. The coach can perform a validation check by asking questions such as:
   - What have you learned?
   - What were the most important insights?
   - What is the central issue of what you have learned?
   - Have you learned what you wanted to?

The manager can find the answers to the following questions in the following statement: 'After practicing giving feedback, I know what I have to do, it feels good and I now do it more often than before. I have investigated how effective my feedback is by talking to my employees and asking them about their experiences. They indicated that the feedback was positive and pleasant. I have therefore learned what I wanted to learn.' If the validation has taken place and the manager is satisfied with the results, then the next step can be taken: determining what the manager will need in the future to maintain the achieved results.

2   *Maintenance:* In the second step, the manager determines how he can perpetuate the new behaviour and insights in the future. Within e-coaching, this is quite a simple process, as all of the information (the entire coaching dialogue) has been recorded in writing. To carry out this step in a structured manner, the manager simply has to review this information. The coach can ask the manager to make an inventory of all the important things that he has learned. In this example, the question could be posed as follows: 'Create a summary of the most important things you have learned about giving feedback. Note down how you gained these new insights and who was involved. Subsequently, consider what (and who) you will need in order to instil these insights in your thought processes.' By writing a summary, the manager crystallizes all of the important steps from the coaching programme. He can then hang the document on his office wall as a reminder. Furthermore,

the manager agrees to contact the coach in six weeks' time to evaluate how he has put the new insights into practice.

3   *Enact:* The third and final step begins once the previous steps have been completed to the satisfaction of both parties and the manager is ready to proceed without the coach's help. With the objective achieved, the coaching programme draws to a close. The new insights and behaviour have been instilled in the manager's natural behavioural patterns and he has a clear picture of what he needs in order to continue along this new path. At the very end, the coach may also ask the manager to carry out an evaluation of the coaching. The programme is concluded, any remaining payments are made, and the coach and manager go their separate ways.

8.2 Summary

In this chapter, we described how the Accelerated Behavioural Change model for e-coaching can be applied in practice. A step-by-step method was given for the three stages (Analyse, Internalize and Sustain) by means of a practical example. During every step of every stage, example questions were provided that the coach can ask to help the client gain the necessary insights. We also showed how the ABC model can be used as a basis for the design and structure of the coaching programme. By using the ABC model as a basis, you can conduct a coaching programme that will realize concrete, sustainable behavioural change. Once stage 2 of the ABC model has been properly conducted and applied, enduring behavioural change will follow. However, this is only possible if the communication between the coach and client is conducted effectively and efficiently. In order to ensure this, we have developed the eCP method. This method consists of two processes: one that analyses the client's messages and one that allows the coach to optimize all communication sent to the client. In the next chapter, we will describe how the eCP method can be applied in practice.

9

THE ECOACHPRO METHOD IN PRACTICE

In this chapter, we will show you how the eCoachPro (eCP) method can be used as a basis for the text-based communication within e-coaching programmes. The eCP method can be applied at every stage of the ABC model in order to ensure efficient and successful communication.

The eCP method consists of two successive processes. The first process analyses the client's communication, while the second process optimizes the coach's communication. The method relates to all written communication as part of the coaching process (e.g. e-mail, chat and text messages). For a description of the eCP method's theoretical foundations, see Chapter 6. In this chapter, we explain the concrete steps that must be taken at every stage of e-coaching programmes to ensure efficient and effective written communication.

Finally, we will give a summary of other communication-related matters that may be of importance when writing messages to clients. In this chapter, the emphasis is once again on the practical application of the method in the coaching process, so there will be only limited reference to the theoretical side of the method. For a more detailed description of theory behind the eCP method, see Chapter 6.

9.1 eCP method process 1: Communication from the client

Process 1 consists of three steps that analyse the communication from the client. These steps are:

- Step 1: Deciding to (re)act
- Step 2: Formulating the acknowledgement/compliment
- Step 3: Conducting thorough linguistic analysis

9.1.1 Step 1: Deciding whether to (re)act

In principle, the client initiates the communication within a coaching programme when s/he decides to enlist the services of a coach. This can consist of a degree of exploration with a view to initiating a coaching programme, although it is possible that the coaching programme begins immediately upon the first message. Whatever happens, the eCP method can be used from the very start. To optimally apply the method, it is important that you take your time. We therefore discourage briefly scanning through the client's messages upon receipt and then rushing yourself to send an immediate response. When you get a message, make sure you take the time to read it through carefully and let it sink in. In practice, the best way to do this is to read it, close it for a while and then reread it later. You can then decide whether or not to respond depending on the content, time available and any agreements you have made with the client. The first step upon receiving a message is therefore deciding whether to respond now or later. This is a step that many beginner coaches find difficult, as it is hard to suppress the natural tendency to read and analyse the message straight away (see Chapter 7).

If you decide not to respond straight away, then don't read the message in too much detail: close it and schedule a time to deal with it. If you analyse it straight away but don't write a response, then the content of the message will bounce around your mind until you eventually put it in writing. As a result, you can end up thinking too much about the programme. If you have enough time to properly analyse and respond to the message, then go on to step 2.

9.1.2 Step 2: Formulating the acknowledgement/compliment

Once you have decided to take the time to respond, it is important that you don't start analysing the text straight away. This is because once you start to analyse, it can be difficult to maintain sufficient distance from the details. You need a more general view of the message in order to get a positive first impression. What we mean by this is that by reading the message from a non-analytical perspective, you can perceive and feel what strikes you as positive about the message. This positive first impression is necessary in order to select the right acknowledgement or compliment to give, which is one of the most important aspects of your reaction. In this step, you will formulate the compliment that you will use in the opening line of your response. Skipping this step and devising a compliment after the analytical stage can be difficult, as once you have analysed the message, you have a fixed idea of its content. Skipping this step and leaving it until later is a mistake that e-coaches frequently make.

Compliments: a vital communication tool

Continual positive reinforcement in the form of compliments is the oil that helps the coaching relationship run smoothly. However, in F2F sessions, compliments during the interaction can disrupt the dialogue. The reason for this is that during interpersonal communication, both parties seek equality and harmony, and compliments can unbalance this feeling of equality. In order to restore the equality, the compliment is then underplayed, watered down or simply rejected, either verbally or otherwise. This reaction mainly occurs when there is a social context, with the coach and client talking face-to-face. This is less of a factor in e-mail communication due to its asynchronous nature and the physical distance between the parties, which creates a degree of social anonymity. As a result, the client can take the compliment without feeling the need to immediately redress the balance of power in the coaching relationship. Social anonymity therefore enables the compliment to have the desired effect: strengthening the coach–client relationship and reinforcing the client's development.

The client will look forward to the coach's messages, as they will always contain something positive. An additional advantage of e-compliments is that they are recorded in writing, so they can be reread at a later date. The positive impact of the compliment can therefore be maintained over time by repeated reading.

Tips for creating effective e-compliments:

- Be sincere: the truth gives a compliment extra power.
- Write in the first person: write the compliment using the words 'I' and 'me' so it is clear who is giving the compliment.
- Mention behaviour: the most effective compliments address specific behaviour displayed by the client.
- Make a positive observation: a compliment includes an observation by the coach combined with a positive assessment.
- Mention what happens to you as a coach while reading the clients work (i.e. Your message brings a smile to my face)
- Write in the present tense: compliments written in the present tense have a more dynamic and motivational effect.

The compliment must be based on your first impression of the message: in your eyes, what has the client done that strikes you as something remarkable or that moves something inside of you? What is noticeably positive about the effort made and/or results achieved? If you can't immediately think of a sincere compliment, then give the client recognition by thanking them for their quick response or their effort. But be careful: although thanking the client for their message is a form of recognition, it is certainly not a compliment. Compliments are the most powerful form of positive reinforcement in the learning process. The following text box gives examples of effective compliments. Once you have formulated an effective compliment, it is time to progress to step 3.

Spotlight: Giving e-compliments

Giving e-compliments is a basic technique that can be used during any stage of the coaching process and at any desired time. Depending on availability, you can use text messages, e-mail, chat programmes or other Internet applications to give compliments. For example, compliments can be sent by e-mail following an F2F coaching session, or even as a replacement for F2F sessions (in the case of e-coaching). You can also send compliments by text message when clients successfully complete exercises.

Compliment 1: After a reflection report

A coach wrote the following compliment to a manager conducting an assignment in the workplace. The manager's coaching objective was to improve the quality of the relationship between employees and customers. The compliment was sent via e-mail.

> 'Firstly, I'd like to say that I admire you for actively seeking feedback. I'm also impressed that you recognize how not doing so causes you problems in your interpersonal contact. That takes guts and self-awareness. Well done!'

Compliment 2: Following an F2F session

During a coaching session, a client said that as a result of an assignment, he opened up to his wife and shared his experiences with her. The coach recognized that this was a big step for the client. As a result, the coach sent the following text message to the client the day after:

> 'Looking back on our session yesterday, I realize that your assignment this week has been difficult for you. It was very brave to open up to your wife like that and show vulnerability. You really have made a great breakthrough and I look forward to our next session.'

In both cases, the compliment is written in the first person and the coach compliments specific things that the client has done. The coach therefore expresses what he thinks and gives his/her seal of approval.

9.1.3 Step 3: Conducting thorough linguistic analysis

In order to sufficiently 'listen' to your client during the e-mail coaching process, you must carry out thorough linguistic analysis on every message that the client sends. The written content of the message is the only information available to the coach. The main question you have to answer is '*What does my client wish to achieve by sending this message?*'

Once you work out the answer to this question, you can take action to support the client in the pursuit of their goals. In order to figure out what the client wishes to achieve, you must correctly interpret the message. Generally, people read far more into written messages than is actually stated in the text. Although this is a natural human response, coaches must be aware of their own filters and avoid loose interpretations of the text. An important aspect of all coach training programmes is to raise coaches' awareness of how their own convictions and assumptions can hinder the coaching process. This is also the case for our e-coach training. Again and again, we have to emphasize the importance of eliminating your own filters and beliefs from the analysis process.

Another problem that coaches can have when interpreting clients' messages is that they take the information too literally. The content of messages are usually not entirely explicit in their meaning: you can often read a great deal between the lines. The process of accurately interpreting the meaning of messages is also known as *close reading*. It means that you not only focus on the meaning of the words in the message, but that you also analyse and interpret the text within the context of both the message itself and the coach–client relationship. This helps to gain deeper insight into the meaning of the text and enables more accurate interpretation.

9.2 Analysis using speech acts

When analysing a message, it is important to find a balance between a loose interpretation and a literal interpretation. If the analysis is not conducted properly, a suitable response cannot be given. You therefore run the risk of missing the point completely. This can also happen during F2F sessions, but it is much easier and quicker to put right. Due to the asynchronicity of e-mail coaching, misunderstandings are more complicated to clear up. To carry out a structured, sentence-by-sentence analysis, the eCP method makes use of 'speech acts' (see Chapter 6 for a detailed explanation). By splitting up the client's message into separate speech acts, you can get a more objective perspective of what the client is saying. As we explained earlier in the book, there are five categories of speech acts:

1 Assertives: The client gives information about the situation.
2 Directives: The client is trying to influence your actions.
3 Expressives: The client is communicating how they feel.
4 Commissives: The client makes promises or commitments.
5 Declaratives: The client is making categorical statements.

In the following text box, you can find an explanation of each category:

Spotlight: Thorough linguistic analysis via speech acts

Upon receiving an e-mail from a client, you can use the five categories of speech acts to analyse the message on a paragraph-by-paragraph or even sentence-by-sentence basis. You can also use this kind of analysis to evaluate your own messages to the client. The following is an explanation of each category of speech acts, illustrated with examples from the client's perspective.

- *Assertives:* These are speech acts that the client uses to say something about their reality. Examples of assertives are statements, beliefs, convictions, descriptions, explanations, conclusions, observations and assumptions. The following sentence is an example of an assertive used by a client: 'I've blown my chances of a good working relationship with John, as he took my feedback completely the wrong way.' Another example in which the client compliments the coach is 'In your last e-mail, you explained the best way that I could plan my presentation, and that really helped me.'
- *Directives:* These speech acts indicate that the client is trying to influence the coach's behaviour. Examples include requests, questions, warnings and advice. It is possible to influence both verbal behaviour (e.g. asking for information) and non-verbal behaviour (e.g. requesting specific action). An example of an information request is 'I would appreciate it if you could give me some information about giving feedback.' An example of a warning or recommendation is 'As you've already noticed, I'm a very sensitive person, so I hope you'll take this into account.'
- *Expressives:* These speech acts sincerely communicate the client's inner state, i.e. what they think and how they feel. Examples include gratitude, congratulations, sorrow, greetings, apologies and welcomes. An example of gratitude is 'I'd like to thank you for your last message, it really helped.' An example of an apology is 'Oh I'm sorry, I completely forgot to write my reflection report yesterday.'
- *Commissives:* Speech acts in this category relate to promises, oaths and guarantees. Commissives indicate that an obligation has been created. Examples include promises, vows, commitments, agreements, guarantees and threats. An example of a promise is 'I promise that I'll e-mail you at least twice this week.' An example of an agreement is 'Before next week, I'll give feedback to two people in my team.'
- *Declaratives:* These speech acts categorically assert a status or condition effective as of the moment that the speech act is performed. In other words, something has changed once the declaration has been made. An example is 'You now have my undivided attention.'

By identifying each speech act that the client uses, you get a clearer picture of the client's needs. A message containing several directives indicates that the client needs something from you and is trying to influence you. For example, they may ask you a question, request information or ask you to change something about the way you work. With directive-laden messages, it is important that you acknowledge the client's needs. When a client's message contains a lot of assertives, they are trying to get across how they see their reality. In these messages, the coach will find a lot of convictions, statements and conclusions. When clients use assertives that contain assumptions and/or convictions, the coach must address them and help the client to scrutinize these presumptions.

Every message that the coach receives will provoke emotions and feelings. Even questions containing nothing but directives can result in a strong emotional reaction. By examining whether expressives are combined with assertives in the message, you can more objectively assess whether the client explicitly states the emotion or if it is simply your interpretation. Expressives – and sometimes assertives – are speech acts that clearly display a particular emotion or feeling, such as 'It was exciting', 'It scared me', and 'It makes me happy'. The client is both expressing an emotion and stating a fact about their reality. When a coach receives a message with lots of expressives, it is important that the coach acknowledges the client's emotions. This shows you are listening and that you value the client's feelings. Sometimes you can even deduce which speech acts the client has used solely from your own reaction.

If you notice that you switch into 'help' mode, i.e. your automatic reaction is to support the client by giving explanations, advice or solutions, then there are probably a lot of directives and expressives in the message. The coach must then choose which points to address and which to omit or delay. However, you must always recognize the client's emotions. In step 4 of the coach's communication (see Section 9.3), we describe how to react to clients' messages using linguistic analysis.

As this method requires sentence-by-sentence linguistic analysis of every message, you might think that it would take much longer than traditional F2F coaching. And for coaches who have never used the method before, you would be right. However, once you gain experience with the method and learn to apply it structurally, the amount of time required decreases dramatically and the process of speech–act analysis becomes increasingly natural.

9.3 eCP method process 2: Communication from the coach

Process 2 consists of five steps that help coaches to optimize the messages they send to their clients. The steps are as follows:

- Step 1: Determine the core content (ABC model).
- Step 2: Decide which medium to use.
- Step 3: Formulate the core content (Language strategies).
- Step 4: Structure the message.
- Step 5: Check the message (Grice).

9.3.1 Step 1: Determine the core content (ABC model)

During process 1, you took the time to work on the client's message, formulate a compliment (or acknowledge the client in another way) and analyse the message. Now you are faced with the most difficult part of e-coaching: Which parts of the message do you respond to? Which needs should you address? What should be the key focus of your response? Clients can write extensively about the experiences, thoughts and feelings they encounter and go into great detail about the exercises and assignments set. As a result, the coach's tendency is to try and address everything the client says. However, that simply isn't practical in e-coaching, so you have to make targeted decisions. These decisions must relate to the predetermined road map that was set in accordance with the ABC model and the main coaching objective. At all times, the overarching aim is to realize the main objective. Throughout every stage of the ABC model, you must determine which actions are required in order to progress towards the coaching objective. The coach must continuously ensure that the client follows the predefined road map. When devising questions to put to the client, ask yourself whether the question truly gets you nearer to realizing the coaching objective or how it helps you to understand the client better. In e-coaching, you must always put the needs of the client first, so the question you ask yourself would be phrased as follows: 'What do I truly need in order to achieve the coaching objective together with the client?' As everything is written down, it is easier to stay on course, as you can review any information you are unsure about. Of course, slight detours are often useful to gain extra insight and depth, but the coach must always watch over the client and ensure they don't stray too far from the path. Depending on the stage of the coaching process and the needs of the client, and always in accordance with the coaching objective, the coach will determine what the core content of the message should be. You can then progress to the next step: accurately formulating the core content.

9.3.2 Step 2: Decide which medium to use

In Chapter 2, we explained how the communication medium used defines the type of coaching. There are many different communication media available for e-coaching, and depending on the message sent, the coach can decide which medium to use for their response (in accordance with the agreements in the coaching agreement – see Chapter 11). Once you have determined what the core content of your message will be (in step 1), then you can decide which medium should be used to communicate your message to the client. For example, if you have deduced that your client needs a sparring partner, then you could recommend telephone, video or chat coaching. If you came to the conclusion that the client needs to be spurred into action or given a quick confidence boost, then you could send a text message. If you need to send a lengthier message, then an e-mail is the best solution. The following steps apply only to the media that make use of the written word.

9.3.3 Step 3: Formulate the core content (language strategies)

If you chose to use send an e-mail or text message in step 2, then you now have to write the message. The way you write the message is the decisive factor in the success of the coaching. As the coaching process continues, the professional relationship grows stronger, and as we explained in Chapter 6, the coach–client relationship is vital to the coaching process. In e-coaching, the way you formulate your message can strengthen the relationship, although it can also damage it. The tone of your messages is an essential factor, and the correct tone depends to a large degree on the amount of 'social distance' between you and your client. The closer you are, the more direct you can be in your messages. Direct messages tend to be more concise. If you have only recently started the coaching process and there is still a degree of social distance between you, then you should use more positive language means focused on the relationship to soften the impact of your messages. Linguistic strategies can help you achieve the right tone in your messages. For more detailed explanation of linguistic strategies, see Chapter 6.

Using linguistic strategies

There are many different linguistic strategies that you can use to optimize the content and structure of your messages. Depending on the client's needs, you can choose a different strategy for each paragraph, or even for each sentence. Choosing the right linguistic strategy is decisive in determining the quality of your message. In order to make the right choice, you must first estimate the status of your professional relationship with the client. How much social distance is between you? There are three different groups of strategies that you can use for e-coaching communication, and the right one to use depends on the degree of social distance between you and the client. The three categories are:

Group 1: Direct with positive language means focused on the relationship

Is there still a degree of unfamiliarity between you and your client or are there still sensitive issues that shouldn't be broached? If so, carefully consider your client's needs and select a bridge-building strategy. This strategy is designed to reduce the social distance between coach and client. The message is clear and unambiguous, but it also shows you are sensitive to the client's needs. The goal is to establish a sense of equality with the client in order to reduce the degree of social distance and bring you closer together. This category contains fifteen specific linguistic strategies geared towards reducing social distance (see also Figure 6.1):

- Strategy 1: Pay attention to your client
- Strategy 2: Exaggerate
- Strategy 3: Emphasize the client's involvement in the dialogue

- Strategy 4: Address the client appropriately and create solidarity
- Strategy 5: Seek agreement
- Strategy 6: Avoid disagreement
- Strategy 7: Assume/offer/confirm a common perspective
- Strategy 8: Use humour
- Strategy 9: Confirm or presume knowledge of and attentiveness for your client's needs
- Strategy 10: Offer or promise something
- Strategy 11: Be optimistic
- Strategy 12: Involve both yourself and your client in the activity
- Strategy 13: Give or ask for reasons
- Strategy 14: Assume or confirm reciprocity
- Strategy 15: Give gifts of sympathy, understanding, co-operation and compliments

These strategies are frequently used in the first stage of the coaching process (the Analyse stage of the ABC model), as you don't yet know the client very well. Another technique that will help you get closer to the client is to mirror his/her use of language as much as possible, i.e. use the same words and terminology that the client uses. For example, if the client usually uses the word 'boss', then copy that instead of using words like 'manager' or 'supervisor'. By mirroring the client's language, you make them feel like you are on the same page. For examples of the various strategies, see the following text box.

Spotlight: The fifteen linguistic bridge-building strategies

- *Strategy 1:* Pay attention to your client. Be attentive to the other person's needs, emotions and difficulties.
- *Strategy 2:* Exaggerate. By using intonation (CAPITAL LETTERS, **boldface**, *italics*, s p a c e s b e t w e e n l e t t e r s etc.), repetition and intensified words, you can add emphasis to what you are saying.
- *Strategy 3:* Emphasize the client's involvement in the dialogue. Try to involve the client in your words by using their name, asking questions like 'don't you agree?' or 'right?', adding statements such as 'listen...', 'the thing is...', 'I repeat...' or by embroidering the facts for effect. In this way, the dialogue becomes livelier, interactive and helps to boost the client's involvement.
- *Strategy 4:* Address the client appropriately and create solidarity. How you talk to each other is important, and depends to a large degree on the level of social distance, i.e. are you on first-name terms, should you use a more formal or relaxed register etc. You can also use jargon that you both understand to help create a bond of understanding.

- *Strategy 5:* Seek agreement. Refer to issues that you both agree on or have similar views about. For example, you can do this by repeating words that the client has written earlier.

- *Strategy 6:* Avoid disagreement. If there is a difference of opinion, then this difference should either be minimized or not acknowledged at all. By using phrases such as 'in a sense', 'to a degree', 'sort of', 'somewhat' or 'not entirely', you can help scale down any difference of opinion.

- *Strategy 7:* Assume/offer/confirm a common perspective. By this, we mean make small talk. Open your dialogue with 'How was your weekend?' or 'How's the weather with you?' You can also gossip, i.e. say something about your CEO if they've been in the news. Another technique is to put yourself in the other person's place, e.g. 'Yes, I understand how hurtful that would be.'

- *Strategy 8:* Use humour. If you want to make someone feel at ease, make jokes relating to any common ground or values that you have with the client.

- *Strategy 9:* Confirm or presume your knowledge of and attentiveness for your client's needs. In this way, you can show you are sensitive to certain needs that the client has not explicitly stated. For example, to reinforce the bond between you, add phrases such as 'Keep going, you're getting there', 'It'll work out just fine', or 'I'm keeping my fingers crossed for you'.

- *Strategy 10:* Offer or promise something. If you notice that the program is not running smoothly, then you can offer or promise things in exchange for certain action, e.g. 'If you answer these questions now, then I'll get back to you first thing in the morning.'

- *Strategy 11:* Be optimistic. Make requests to the client, but phrase them in a way that shows you are optimistic that the request will be honoured. For example, 'If we keep going at this rate, then we'll achieve the coaching objective in no time!'

- *Strategy 12:* Involve both yourself and your client in the activity. Instead of using 'I' and 'you', use the first-person plural 'we'. In this way, you emphasize the bond with your client and boost the level of co-operation. The example in strategy 11 is also an example of strategy 12.

- *Strategy 13:* Give or ask for reasons. You can also deepen your client's involvement by giving reasons and well-founded arguments. By giving reasons and formulating them as though the client accepts them too, you can help reinforce your solidarity with the client. You can also ask questions, such as 'Why not do this?', although, you must bear in mind that you are a coach, not an advisor.

- *Strategy 14:* Assume or confirm reciprocity. Hold each other to mutual rights and responsibilities, e.g. 'I have been open and honest with you, I hope you will respond in kind.'

- *Strategy 15:* Give gifts of sympathy, understanding, co-operation and compliments. This relates to needs that have been explicitly stated. Use these gifts when you know that they will influence the client. The need for recognition and validation is a basic human need. Using compliments and positive reinforcement when the client encounters new experiences is a powerful tool in learning new behaviour and making it stick.

Group 2: Direct without positive language means

Once you have got close enough to your client and the social distance has been sufficiently reduced, then you can make increasing use of more direct and succinct phraseology. Messages in this style are generally brief, to the point, goal-oriented, and concise. This style is suitable once the coach and client have built up a good professional relationship. However, be careful not to be too blunt.

Group 3: No speech act

One of the most common pitfalls for e-coaches is the desire to address every single point raised in the client's message (see step 1). An essential skill in e-coaching is to avoid mentioning certain things or temporarily putting them off. Not mentioning particular matters is a strategic choice, and therefore a perfectly valid linguistic strategy. By only responding to parts of the message that are relevant to the coaching program, you ensure that the process remains on course. Another reason to avoid responding to a particular part of a message is to prevent discussions. The asynchronicity of e-mail communication makes it difficult to conduct lengthy written debates. It is therefore advisable to avoid provoking discussions. However, saying nothing about a particular issue can sometimes damage or disrupt the coaching process. If this is the case, try to bring the issue into the discussion by using the measures for positive relationship-oriented action.

9.3.4 Step 4: Structure the message

The eCP method uses a standard message format, giving the coach a tool for creating structured messages. You therefore don't have to spend time deciding how to respond to your client's messages. It also makes it easier to check your messages to ensure you haven't forgotten anything. Every written message contains a number of essential elements that facilitate effective and efficient communication. The structure consists of the following five elements:

1   Header
2   Opening with acknowledgement (acknowledgement/compliment)

3   Core content
4   Conclusion with expectation management (activate and motivate)
5   Footer

1. Header

The header includes the address of both sender and recipient, the date and time at which the e-mail was sent, the subject and the greeting. Most e-mail programs and online working environments automatically display the name of the sender and the time that the message was sent. If this is the case, you need only add a greeting. You can vary your greetings, and it is also a good idea to mirror the greetings used by the client. For example, if the client opens their messages with 'Dear (name)', then it is advisable to start your e-mails in the same way. As the social distance reduces, you can switch to greetings such as 'Hello', 'Hi' or 'Hey'.

2. Opening with acknowledgement (compliment)

After the greeting, your opening sentence should acknowledge the client's efforts. You can do this by naming specific actions or giving a compliment about results achieved or other work that the client has done. Your message must always relate to the client's message. If your e-mails start with a compliment, the client looks forward to them as it gives them positive energy and motivation. We already discussed ideas on how to give recognition in step 2 of process 1 (Section 9.1.2).

3. Core content

The core content of the message will have already been determined in the previous steps. It consists of two important elements: it must reflect upon and/or give feedback regarding the client's last message, and it must pose another question or assignment that signifies the client's next step in the coaching process. You can also give or recommend additional information to help them with future assignments. For example, you could send a document with background information about a particular subject. You can also answer any questions that the client may have asked in their last message.

4. Conclusion with expectation management (activate and motivate)

Towards the end, you indicate that the ball is now in the client's court and you let them know what you expect from them. You could then be forgiven for putting your feet up and waiting for the client to get to work. However, if you want to maximize the advantages of e-coaching, then it is advisable to state a clear set of expectations. This motivates the client to put their words into action and challenges them to take the next step in the coaching process. Be as specific as possible when devising your expectations, but make sure you don't sound too demanding. Always end your message with a positive and motivational closing line. This could express how well you think the client is doing or how quickly the client is making progress. You could also close the message with a promise.

5. Footer

Here, you end the message with a standard greeting or a variation that is appropriate to the professional relationship. An e-mail signature can also be added, which contains information about the sender.

This format is not set in stone, and a degree of variation is possible. However, it has been shown that messages beginning with a compliment or recognition can help strengthen the coach–client relationship. It has also been shown that ending messages with a motivational closing line encourages clients to take action quicker and keeps them coming back. It is therefore advisable to include these two elements in your e-mails, particularly at the start of the coaching process.

Once you have written your message, you can progress to the final step.

9.3.5 Step 5: Check the message

The last step in the process is checking your message. Questions that you should ask yourself during this step include:

- Have I focused on the right issues?
- Have I said what I wanted to say?
- Have I stuck to the point?
- Does the message meet the client's needs?
- Have I included a sincere compliment?
- Does the message include a clear assignment or question that galvanizes the client into action?
- Am I asking too many questions?

Although this step is of vital importance, coaches often skip it. This is because people are not very good at checking their own work. To solve this problem, the eCP method makes use of the four Gricean Maxims for goal-oriented communication (see Section 6.7). These rules help optimize the effectiveness of your communication. The Gricean Maxims are as follows:

1 *Relation:* Is what you have written relevant?
2 *Quantity:* How well do you express yourself? Make sure you avoid using too few or too many words. Say only what you need to say. Avoid expressing yourself too forcefully or too ineffectively. Be frugal with your words, as every unnecessary word increases the likelihood of misinterpretation.
3 *Quality:* Is what you are writing correct? In principle, what you say must be

the truth. Don't say things you don't believe and don't say anything you can't back up with evidence.

4   *Clearness:* Don't use obscure, unclear or indirect language. Be straightforward.

By using these four maxims to check every message, you will make your messages shorter, clearer and more powerful.

9.4 Other aspects of written messages

In the previous section, we explained how to formulate a message to your client. The eCP method uses a set format that takes into account all of the specific aspects of online communication. In this section, we will list a number of other points for attention when writing messages to clients. This summary is based on Chapter 3 (E-communication: The New World of Communication) and Chapter 7 (Experiences of E-coaches). The following is an explanation of these three aspects (format, content and additional aspects).

9.4.1 Format

- Be brief and concise: The principle within e-coaching is to write sentences that are as short and as straightforward as possible. In addition to making your message more readable and manageable, it also prevents misunderstandings. Don't use too many commas. The rule of thumb is if there is a comma in a sentence, split it into two separate sentences.
- Write short paragraphs: The paragraphs help to create the structure of the messages. Leave a space between paragraphs to increase readability and clarity.
- Repeat your references: If you refer to a particular sentence or statement in the client's message, repeat it by simply copying and pasting it into your message.
- Numbered lists: If you use a list to summarize something, number each element in the list. This increases the clarity and readability of the summary. If you split a question into three sub questions, you should also number the sub questions.
- Avoid abbreviations: Professionals in every field make use of technical jargon and abbreviations. While this is useful for communication between fellow professionals, it can be confusing for your clients. If you have to use abbreviations when contacting your client, make sure you explain them properly and indicate that you will be using this abbreviation in future communication.
- Try not to shout: Overuse of capital letters, underlining and/or exclamation marks can make it look like you are shouting. If you want to draw attention to something, then use **boldface**, <u>underlined text</u> or *italics*. Carefully consider why you want to draw attention to that particular word and what effect it will have on the client. It can be very useful in certain situations, such as to reinforce a compliment (e.g. 'WOW – I'm impressed!!!')

- Use correct spelling and grammar: A coach's written messages effectively function as business cards. If your messages look unprofessional, you look unprofessional. It is therefore vital that you use correct spelling and grammar. Naturally, this doesn't apply to the client. If the client uses poor spelling and grammar, then you must not draw attention to this.

9.4.2 Content

Be careful with the following matters:

- Sharing personal experiences: Coaching is all about the client. Their accounts and experiences are the central focus of the coaching process. You must therefore avoid giving too many examples from your own life. Minimize your use of the words 'I' and 'me'. It is possible to share a personal experience here and there if it is relevant to the coaching process, but you must introduce it properly to the dialogue and explain why it is relevant.
- Assumptions, suppositions and interpretations: As coaches, we are trained to listen without prejudice. However, in practice, we make more assumptions than we think. Even experienced coaches can be guilty of this, as we discovered from some of the messages sent during our e-coach training programs. It is therefore something that every coach must guard against throughout their career. The advantage of written communication is that you can read through and check your messages before sending them. If a particular assumption or interpretation is relevant to a particular message, consequence or exercise, make sure you first check its accuracy with the client.
- Clichés: These can also come across differently in black and white. What would be a throwaway comment in a face-to-face conversation can sometimes irritate the client in writing.
- Identifying causes: In the field of social and behavioural science, it is practically impossible to prove causal links. You can have reasons to believe there may be a link, but categorically stating that A causes B is extremely presumptuous. You should therefore avoid doing so at all costs.

9.4.3 Additional aspects

Other factors include:

- Asking too many questions: As the saying goes, one question equals one answer, three questions equal no answers. It is natural for coaches to ask questions. After all, questions are one of the most powerful tools in the coach's arsenal. However, in e-coaching, there is only room for one question per e-mail, or two at the very most. If you do ask two questions, then make sure you number them to make them optimally clear to the client. The limit on the number of questions means that you have to think very carefully about exactly what you want to ask. You should therefore scrutinize why you want to ask certain questions. Are they to give you better understanding or are they of relevance to the client? By employing this method, you will improve the quality of the questions you ask.

- Sharing knowledge: At various moments throughout the coaching process, you may wish to provide the client with information. This can be done in many ways, such as via an article in a journal, a link to a website or a video. However, it is important that this information is not included in the dialogue. It should be provided separately (for example, as an e-mail attachment) to ensure that it does not distract from the dialogue. The same thing applies for assignments and exercises: send them separately. By distinguishing between the dialogue and all other information, the dialogue remains fully focused on the core content. The online coaching environment that we use (Pluform.com) is specially designed to facilitate this, offering special functions to improve the efficiency and success of your e-coaching. See Chapter 10 for more information about Pluform.com.
- Humour or irony: These are frequently taken the wrong way when used in writing. If this could be the case, make sure you use emoticons or other symbols to make it clear you are joking.
- Other linguistic devices: The absence of non-verbal signals within written communication can be partially compensated by using symbols and other linguistic devices such as emoticons, sound words, emphasis fonts and action words. See Section 3.3 for a summary of the various linguistic tools at your disposal.

9.5 Summary

In this chapter, we described how the eCoachPro method can be applied in practice. The aim of the eCP method is to optimize the efficiency and effectiveness of the coaching communication. The method consists of two successive processes. The first process contains the steps you must take to analyse the client's messages and the second process helps the coach to formulate messages to the client. The steps in the first process are 1) receipt of the message from the client, 2) formulation of a compliment and 3) thorough linguistic analysis. The steps in the second process are 1) determine the core content 2) decide which medium to use, 3) formulate the core content, 4) structure the message and 5) check the message. These steps provide coaches with an easy-to-use tool that ensures successful communication within e-coaching programs. It is therefore important to apply this method during all stages of the ABC model.

Now you are familiar with the ABC model and the eCP method, the next step is to determine what technology to use. Ultimately, this technology is what makes the process of e-coaching possible. In the next chapter, we will explain the importance of reliable and secure technology, as well as highlighting a few things to look out for when using various technological solutions.

10

E-COACHING TECHNOLOGY

The 'e' of e-coaching stands for electronic. This indicates that technology is a decisive factor in this type of coaching. The availability of technology – the medium that enables the communication – can make or break the effectiveness of e-coaching. Obviously, for telephone coaching, a telephone is required with either an analogue or digital connection. For all other types of e-coaching, you need a computer, smartphone or tablet with an Internet connection at the very least, and you may also require extra software. Different software is available depending on which type of e-coaching you employ. If you choose synchronous communication, you will need chat, video–chat and/or Internet-telephony programmes. For asynchronous communication, e-mail programmes, webmail, Internet forums, discussion groups and SMS applications could be used. Of course, you could also choose a combination of these options. The most important factor is that they must be user-friendly, accessible, reliable and secure from the perspective of both coach and client. This chapter addresses the various important issues involved when selecting e-coaching software. We will also introduce Pluform.com as an example of a digital coaching environment.

10.1 Professional Internet applications: advantages and disadvantages

10.1.1 Free software

There is a huge amount of free software available for online communication. Well-known examples include Outlook, Google Buzz, Windows Messenger (MSN), Skype, Twitter, Chatzilla and WhatsApp. In addition, there are free networking websites that combine different communication tools. Examples of these websites are Facebook, MySpace, Google+ and LinkedIn, which are generic programs used for various social and communication purposes. Often, there is little to no cost involved in using these sites. As they are free to access, everyone can use them. For this reason, coaches rarely specialize in the use of these programs, they just incorporate them as an extra service for their clients. The disadvantage of these programs is that they are difficult to adjust to suit specific e-coaching processes or objectives.

Paying with data

Another – often invisible – disadvantage of these free programs is that the providers collect the users' data. This personal information is then sold to enable targeted advertising. The following is a simplified explanation of how this works:

> When you use free programs such as Google's Gmail, all e-mails you send and receive are saved, scanned and stored on Google's servers. Furthermore, Google saves all of the searches you have made using the Google search engine. Google can also track your Internet usage using cookies that record your online activity. All of this information is collected by Google and used to communicate personalized advertisements to you. This means that when visiting a website, adverts will appear that may be specifically of interest to you. Other major software companies such as Microsoft, Apple and Yahoo also use similar techniques to collect personal information from you via free products and services.

The more free programs the coach and client use, the greater the chance that the content of the coaching process will be used as input for advertising campaigns.

10.1.2 Digital learning environment (DLE)

In order to increase the user-friendliness and reliability of software, various market players have developed special digital environments that combine many different communication channels. Coaches who specialize in particular types of e-coaching in their professional practice are making more and more use of these special online environments. Digital environments are secure websites in which coach and client can work together. Digital coaching environments are simplified versions of digital learning environments (DLEs). DLEs are programs or websites that help to structure and conduct flexible remote learning and supervision. Although there is no teacher–student relationship within e-coaching, digital coaching environments do involve similar learning processes. It is therefore no surprise that various providers of DLE systems also operate in the coaching sector, offering special digital environments suitable for coaching. In addition, there are also developers who create online working environments in line with the New World of Work, in which online communication plays a key role. As a result, coaches can choose from an increasingly wide variety of digital systems in order to support their coaching practice.

10.1.3 Professional providers

There are many providers of digital coaching environments. These include:

- Covocative.com
- CoachAccountable.com
- Pluform.com
- CoachingCloud.com
- Covocative.com
- JournalEngine.com
- Lifecoachhub.com
- LPScocoon.de
- My360plus.com
- ProReal.co.uk

The advantage of using a digital coaching environment instead of separate communication programs is that all information relating to a particular coaching process can be stored in and retrieved from the same place. You can also create a secure location on the Internet that only the coach and client can access. A frequent disadvantage is that many digital coaching environments do not sufficiently take into account the unique nature of the coaching process. Two characteristics of most digital working environments are as follows:

1   *Technology oriented:* Working environments in this category tend to focus on technology for technology's sake. In short, this means that sophisticated technology and functionalities are added simply because they are technically possible, not because they promote ease of use or facilitate the user experience. The interface is often cluttered due to the multitude of functionalities that are rarely used, if at all. Working environments that are user-oriented focus on the user rather than the sophistication of the technology. This means that the needs of the end users serve as the decisive factor in how the technology is created. A simple rule of thumb is that the simpler and clearer the interface, the more user-friendly it is.

2   *Supply-driven and in line with the e-learning principle:* Many digital coaching environments are not specifically designed for the purposes of coaching. They are often digital learning environments that require a large degree of self-sufficiency from the participant/student/client. The user must independently follow procedures in order to achieve a specific goal. The courses involve modules that are completed one after another, with supervision provided at certain moments. This is ideal for supply-driven courses or protocol-based programmes intended for learning certain skills, providing therapy etc. In this situation, users follow a predetermined learning path supported by a teacher, mentor, supervisor or coach. This type of digital learning environment therefore focuses on independent learning via assignments and exercises, with

communication media incorporated in order to provide support. This is typical of the e-learning principle. However, coaching is demand-driven rather than supply-driven: every coaching client undergoes a unique process that is tailored to their own personal circumstances and objectives. As a result, the communication process is of greater importance than the completion of assignments or exercises, and it should therefore be the dominant feature of the interface. However, in many digital coaching environments, this is not the case.

10.2 Requirements of a digital coaching environment

When selecting a practical digital coaching environment, it is therefore important to look for one that is both user-oriented and demand-driven. User-friendliness is one of the most vital criteria when selecting a coaching environment, and the following matters should also be taken into consideration:

10.2.1 Privacy

Privacy regarding Internet use is an issue that many people neglect. Everything that we do on the Internet leaves a trail that is difficult to erase. Furthermore, the huge increase in social networking sites such as LinkedIn or Facebook has made it perfectly normal to publish personal information online. The combination of nonchalant sharing of personal information and the difficulty of erasing this information from the Internet means that our privacy is being increasingly encroached upon. E-coaching requires clients to share a great deal of personal information via the Internet. It is the coach's responsibility to ensure that the client's personal information is handled professionally and securely. In the ethical codes of practice of various professional organizations for coaches, you can find guidelines governing the handling of clients' personal information. An example of these rules is that it is not permitted to share a client's personal information with third parties without the client's consent. Another example is that paper files containing information about clients must be locked away. These guidelines, which apply to all coaches registered with the professional organization in question, govern all information gathered during e-coaching programmes. Coaches who make use of e-coaching must make sure that any digital environments used during the coaching process sufficiently safeguard the privacy of their clients at all times.

10.2.2 Security

It is vital that the digital coaching environment used is completely secure and that the information is inaccessible to other parties not involved in the coaching programme. The security of the coaching environment can be organized in a variety of ways. A few examples of these methods include:

- *Username/password:* As standard, protected working environments are secured with a username and password. Only users who know the correct username/password combination can gain access to the secure environment. Nowadays, in addition to this security measure, many websites also use CAPTCHAs.[1] This is a security measure that protects against automated password hackers (*bots*) using characters that are difficult to read. As only a human being could tell which characters are displayed, you effectively have to prove that you are human when logging in.
- *Security certificates:* Websites with a security certificate ensure that all information from the website is sent to the user's computer in encrypted form. These certificates mainly make use of Secure Sockets Layer (SSL). Currently, the SSL protocol is the most frequently used method for encrypting electronic transactions via the Internet. Websites secured in this manner can be recognized by the addition of an 's' in the URL ('http' becomes 'https', with the 's' standing for 'secure'). Security certificates also offer different levels of security. For example, EV SSLs are more extensive versions of SSL certificates, signifying that the applicant has been subjected to extra scrutiny. Websites that possess an EV SSL can be recognized by a green URL bar or green letters in the URL bar. Banks and other organizations that process highly sensitive information particularly use this type of extensive certificate.
- *Two-way identification tools:* With more sophisticated security measures, the user may be asked to enter login codes that differ for each login attempt (i.e. different data is required each time). The user must identify him/herself using information provided by a separate device (known as a reader). Another way of doing this is providing a code via a text message which you then enter during the login process.

The more security measures you use, the more secure your digital environment is. However, you must ensure that the security measures do not detract from the user-friendliness of the digital environment. If users have to go through numerous layers of security when logging in, then they will use the digital environment less frequently. The key is finding a balance between optimal security and maximum user-friendliness.

10.2.3 Storage

All information shared on the Internet is saved on computers. During chat and e-mail coaching programs, large volumes of text are sent and stored in the digital coaching environment (this can also apply to recorded telephone and video coaching sessions). Digital coaching environments must therefore have high-quality systems to ensure that the data cannot be lost. In principle, all of the information is saved on the servers belonging to the provider of the digital coaching environment. It is important to know where these computers are, how their security is organized and what happens if they fail. The servers are usually located in server parks. These are locations in which large numbers of computers are kept, with facilities available to make backups of all information saved on the computers. In general, the provider of the digital working environment will give limited guarantees regarding the accessibility of the computers and the creation of backups. If the provider's computers are kept abroad, then you must take into account that the privacy laws in the country in question may be different.

10.2.4 Use of e-mail

One point of attention is the built-in e-mail programs offered by digital working environments. These e-mail programs enable you to send messages to external e-mail addresses, usually the user's private or business e-mail account. It is important that these e-mails are sent in encrypted form. If this is not the case, then the e-mails can be intercepted and read by third parties. The use of e-mail programs can also raise other privacy issues. By using e-mail programs that send messages to the user's private or business e-mail address, there is a chance that third parties can gain access to the user's inbox. For example, employers technically have access to their employees' e-mail accounts with programs like VNC, LogMeIn, Shadow, SpyAgent, Web Sleuth and Silent Watch. According the *'2007 Electronic Monitoring and Surveillance Survey'* conducted by the American Management Association (AMA) and The ePolicy Institute, 43 per cent of employers are monitoring their employees' e-mail (automatically or manually).

If your coaching client is a manager, then there is a chance that all e-mails sent to them can be read by a secretary or management assistant. Naturally, the content of coaching programmes should remain confidential, so secretaries or assistants should not be able to access the messages. It is therefore advisable to use an e-mail account unrelated to the client's company. Furthermore, if the e-mail address in question is also used for purposes unrelated to the coaching, then the structure and convenience of the coaching programme can be affected because the coaching-related e-mails are mixed in with other e-mails. It is therefore advisable to use digital coaching environments in which all e-mail traffic takes place internally.

10.2.5 Time and location independence

During coaching programmes in which most of the communication is conducted via a digital coaching environment, it is important that the coaching environment is available whenever it is needed. As the frequency of contact significantly contributes to the success of e-coaching, it is essential that you have a stable and continually accessible digital coaching environment. A good digital coaching environment therefore needs to be accessible 24 hours a day, 7 days a week without the need for any extra software or special adjustments to the user's computer. Most providers of digital working environments offer this via a special website that can be used without any extra software or specific computer settings. Providers who guarantee excellent accessibility and availability of their digital working environments therefore enable truly time- and location-independent coaching.

10.2.6 User support

Although most providers wax lyrical about how user-friendly their digital environments are, users still frequently encounter problems. The more technically oriented and supply-oriented the working environment is, the greater the chance that the user will encounter problems. After all, the average user has only limited knowledge of online programs. If problems occur, then it is preferable that the provider of the working environment gives the user the support they need.

Most providers of digital working environments provide technical support in the event of problems or failure of the system, although the speed of this service varies greatly from provider to provider. Some providers offer Service Level Agreements (SLAs), in which the response time to problems is specified. However, this type of support is nearly always limited to the functionality of the digital environment itself. In practice, many problems that users encounter are not always caused by the digital environment itself, but by the user's equipment (computer and/or Internet connection). In such situations, it is preferable that support is given regarding all technical aspects of the digital environment, as this minimizes the risk of stagnating the coaching process.

This extensive technical support can be further supplemented with practical user support. Although most digital environments are structured in a user-friendly manner, limited knowledge of and experience with computers and/or the Internet can make this type of coaching unsuitable for technically challenged coaches or clients. However, you can remove this obstacle by selecting a provider who offers good-quality technical and user support as standard.

10.3 Development of Pluform

As mentioned earlier, in order to provide effective coaching via a digital coaching environment, you must take into account a whole range of preconditions and requirements. For this reason, we have developed our own digital coaching environment that satisfies all of these requirements. This digital coaching environment, named Pluform, is designed to provide optimal support within all kinds of coaching programmes. Depending on the method, approach and type of coaching, you can decide whether to use Pluform for fully online coaching programmes or as a support tool within F2F programmes. For example, exercises within F2F programmes can be set online, and the client can then write up the exercise within the digital environment for the coach to read. Within e-coaching programmes, the coach may decide to conduct all communication within the digital coaching environment.

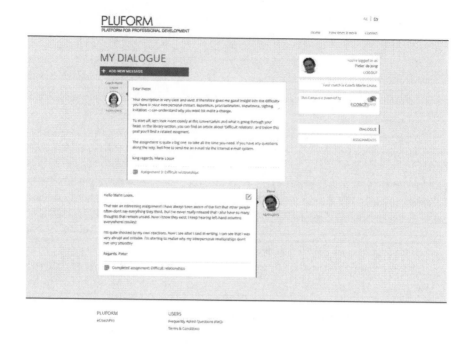

FIGURE 10.1 Pluform Dialogue window

10.3.1 Functionalities of Pluform

Pluform can be used for both synchronous communication (via chat and video) and asynchronous communication (via e-mail and the messaging system). In addition to numerous communication functionalities, Pluform also offers document-editing and storage facilities. The basic functionalities of Pluform are:

- *Dialogue:* This is the central functionality that facilitates both the coach and client to have a written conversation through exchanging messages with each other during the coaching programme. These messages are not sent by means of a standard e-mail format but by means of a chronological messaging format where the entire conversation remains visible within the profile of the coach and client. Using this function neatly and efficiently organizes all communication relating to the core content of the coaching programme. When a message is sent, a notification e-mail is also sent to an external e-mail address belonging to the coach and/or client.
- *Assignments:* This function enables the coach to prepare and add assignments, exercises and/or provide additional information. The client can then use this information to work in the worksheet section.

- *Worksheet:* This function enables the client to write up his/ her assignments and exercises provided by the coach in different worksheets. Clients can also use this function to reflect upon assignments or to keep a diary if desired. The coach has access to the worksheets, enabling him/her to give feedback to the client.
- *Library:* This functionality enables you to build a collection of files that you use in your coaching. If you wish to provide a document, schedule, article or other information to your client, you can upload it here in different file formats.
- *Objectives:* This function enables a solution-oriented approach to achieving the goals. The objectives and/or points for improvement are visibly displayed by means of scale questions. The objectives can be divided into subgoals. At the start of the coaching programme, the client can award a score of 1 to 10 with regard to his/her coaching objective or various aspects of it. Subsequently, the client can reassess their scores for each objective/subgoal at specific time intervals in order to give an up-to-date assessment of their progress. In this way, the client's development is visually displayed and the effectiveness of the coaching programme can be measured.
- *Profile:* This functionality displays the account page with full name, username and status (online or offline). It is also possible to add a photo of the coach and/or client. This photo will be visible within various functions, which helps add a personal touch to the Pluform environment. It also enables the coach to upload photos or other images that could facilitate the coaching process.
- *Coach Badge:* As standard, a Coach Badge is used within the client's digital environment (ClientCampus profile). Upon login, this immediately shows the client who the provider of the coaching environment is (in this case, the coach). The coach can decide to use a different Coach Badge for each ClientCampus profile. The Coach Badge features the company logo and displays other information relating to the coach.

10.3.2 Supplementary Pluform functionalities

In addition to the basic functionalities, Pluform offers a number of extra functions that can support the coaching programme (depending on the license type). An example of these supplementary communication functionalities are as follows:

- *E-mail system:* The internal e-mail system allows users to send standard e-mails to each other as in any other standard e-mail functionality. This is an independent functionality from the dialogue function. The e-mails are not visible in the dialogue section where the actual coaching takes place (see preceding 'Dialogue' paragraph). The coach and client can use the email function for general messages or to introduce new activities. Use the e-mail function for the exchange of all information that doesn't refer to the content of the coaching programme. However, if preferred one may choose to use this function to initiate a coaching programme where the coaching communi-

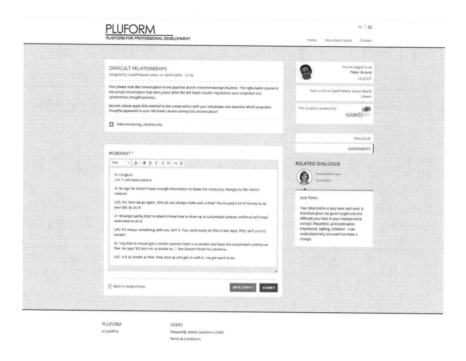

FIGURE 10.2 Pluform Worksheet window

cation is completely conducted in this standard e-mail functionality. To send and receive e-mails via this system, all you have to do is log in to Pluform. The advantages of this system include that it is very simple, it cannot receive or send any spam, and it can be accessed 24/7 from anywhere in the world. The internal e-mail system can also send notifications to the user's external e-mail account (either business or personal) every time they receive an internal e-mail from another Pluform user. Once you get started with Pluform, you can change the notification settings as desired.

- *Chat rooms:* For synchronous communication (i.e. when both coach and client are online), you can use the internal chat program. This chat function enables live chats between the coach and client, the coach and several clients, or several coaches and several clients. Chats can be described as digital conversations in which the words are written rather than spoken. Once the information is typed out and sent, it immediately appears on-screen. The other participant(s) in the conversation do the same, with all contributions visible on-screen to all participants. Pluform offers an open chat room in which all users can chat with each other, and a private chat room for one-on-one conversations between coach and client. No extra software is required to use these chat rooms.

- *SMS system:* The Short Messaging Service (SMS) system enables the coach to send text messages from the Pluform system to the client's mobile phone. This function can supplement the regular coaching programme by giving the client extra motivation. The SMS function can also be used to spur the client into action or to help maintain the client's momentum. Text messages have a high attention value, which makes them a powerful tool for maintaining and optimizing contact with the client. To send text messages within Pluform, all you need to do is log in. Advantages of this system include its simplicity, its 24/7 availability and the ability to send messages internationally as well as domestically (e.g. if the client is away on business). Any text messages sent are saved in the SMS archive in the coach's profile.

All of the text-based functionalities in Pluform enable you to edit the layout and add visual elements. Above many of the text boxes you can find two rows of buttons that can be used to edit your messages. In addition to these editing functions, you can also illustrate your words using emoticons, which are symbols that express specific emotions. Using these symbols, you can visualize particular emotions, behaviour and intentions (e.g. showing that something was a joke) in your written conversation.

10.3.3 Pluform: availability and support

Pluform is entirely web-based and can be operated from any location with access to a computer with an Internet connection. No extra software or special settings are required. Pluform does everything possible to keep all functionalities available 24 hours a day, 7 days a week. A 100 per cent guarantee cannot be given due to the dependence on the Internet and the performance/technology of the computer.

Pluform is also extremely user-friendly thanks to its simple and convenient layout and structure. In order to get the most out of Pluform, a number of manuals are available containing extensive descriptions of the various functions and facilities. If you have any problems when using Pluform, then you can contact user support by phone on weekdays. The user-support helpdesk can assist you in solving any technical or user-related issues.

The utmost care and attention has been paid to ensuring the security, accessibility and user-friendliness of Pluform. Pluform uses a secure environment with an Extended Validation (EV) SSL security certificate. Pluform is secured by a username and password system.

Coaches can only access the campus profiles of their own clients. Clients cannot view each other's profiles. As standard, no personal name or address details, phone numbers or e-mail addresses are made visible in campus profiles. Daily and weekly backups of Pluform are made. These backup files are safely secured and stored for no longer than a month.

10.4 Summary

E-coaching cannot exist without technology. The entire process is conducted online and supported by computers, tablets and/or smartphones. One of the most vital aspects when using technology is the issue of security. Security can be divided into two categories: technological security and the client's peace of mind. It is vital that any software, websites and applications used are secured by means of Extended Validation (EV) SSL security certificates, personal login codes and other security measures. In addition to this, the client must have the assurance that his/her personal information cannot be accessed by third parties. The provision of coaching via free e-mail programs involves extra risk. These risks relate to ownership of the data (nearly all providers of free programs use the user information for advertising purposes), data storage, and other issues. Using a digital coaching environment can eliminate a large number of security and privacy concerns. However, it is still advisable to pay attention to issues such as user-friendliness, security and data ownership. One of the secure coaching environments on the market is Pluform.com. This site was developed from the perspective of the user and offers all kinds of functionalities to support the coaching process.

Now that we are clear about the requirements relating to privacy, security, usage and application of e-coaching technology, we can move on to the next chapter, in which we discuss the remaining preconditions for successful e-coaching.

Note

1   CAPTCHA is an acronym of 'Completely Automated Public Turing test to tell Computers and Humans Apart'.

11

FACILITATING THE E-COACHING PROCESS

In the previous chapters, we explained how the Accelerated Behavioural Change model and the eCoachPro method can be applied in practice. We also showed the importance of technology in their application. Once you know how to apply all of the aspects and instruments of e-coaching, you have laid the foundations for the design and execution of successful e-coaching programmes. However, in addition to these instruments, there are many other aspects that you must master in order to be successful as an e-coach. In this chapter, we will address a wide variety of practical matters relating to the set-up and execution of successful e-coaching programmes. First, we will highlight the important elements in the design stage. We will then introduce a formula for calculating the program fee. Subsequently, we will provide a checklist featuring the 12 most important aspects of e-coaching agreements. The chapter then concludes by explaining how you can properly manage your client's (and your own) expectations regarding the e-coaching process.

11.1 Preparation

Getting started with e-coaching is not as straightforward as it may seem. Although some coaches will simply tell you to get on with it, this book has shown that it's just not as simple as that. It is a different discipline, and as such, a good coach is not necessarily a good e-coach. E-coaching requires a different mindset, a different approach, different skills and a different attitude. You should therefore carefully consider if e-coaching is a useful path to take in your career. Chapter 7 can help you to decide whether e-coaching would be a valuable addition to your coaching practice. If you decide that you still want to train as an e-coach, then this book will serve as excellent preparation.

Most coach-training programmes include a great deal of practical work with regard to coaching skills. After all, the best way to apply new skills in a real-world scenario is to get lots of practice. This is also the case for e-coaching. However, standard coach-training programmes pay very little attention to online coaching. It is therefore advisable to take extra training courses that specifically bring e-coaching to life via theoretical studies, practical exercises, intervision and supervision.

Once you have laid the foundations for your e-coaching practice, you must determine what technology you will use to support it. Technology can both make and break your e-coaching practice, and a reliable and secure technological infrastructure is of vital importance. After all, without information and communication technology (ICT), e-coaching is entirely impossible. You will therefore have to carefully research the various technological solutions available to you. What computer programs will you use? Can you use them for free or are additional costs involved? An equally important factor is the reliability and security of the software. Chapter 10 can help you to decide which applications are most suitable to your needs.

11.2 Designing e-coaching programmes

The ABC model provides the basic structure of e-coaching programmes. Chapters 5 and 8 can help you adjust the ABC model to best suit your style of coaching. You can assess each stage of the model individually, decide how to approach it and choose what tools and technology to use. Just like traditional coaching, e-coaching has to be tailor-made to suit each individual client. As a result, there is no fixed formula that dictates how a standard e-coaching programme is structured. However, in addition to the ABC model, there are many recurring factors that must be determined for each e-coaching programme. These are:

1 Type of coaching (F2F, e-coaching).
2 Medium (F2F, chat, e-mail, telephone, video, text messages).
3 Duration and contact frequency (online and F2F).
4 Coaching techniques and tools (digital availability).

The structure of every e-coaching programme is therefore dependent on the decisions you make for each factor. In the following paragraphs, we will give a brief description of the various options available.

1. Type of coaching

The first decision you have to make is whether to conduct it entirely online or to combine it with F2F sessions (known as a hybrid programme). These hybrid programmes could start with an F2F intake session before continuing exclusively online. If desired, you could choose to arrange multiple F2F sessions or none at all. In our experience, many beginner e-coaches like to work with hybrid programmes, while more experienced e-coaches or e-coaches whose clients live far away usually opt for fully online programmes.

2. Medium

The second decision you must make is the type of e-coaching you will use. Effectively, this simply means selecting the most suitable communication medium. You can choose from e-mail, chat, telephone, video or SMS coaching, or a combination of these. The choices that you make at this stage are largely determined by the coaching objectives. For example, if you want a sparring session with the client with a degree of social anonymity, then chat coaching is the most suitable option. In Chapter 2, we investigated the pros and cons of the various types of e-coaching, so this chapter can help you with this decision. Of course, it is important that you feel at home with the chosen medium. For example, if you don't have much experience with chat programs, make sure you get sufficient practice before using this medium for coaching. The coach must be able to optimally support the client during the coaching process, so it is essential that you possess all of the necessary knowledge and skills.

3. Duration and contact frequency

The third decision relates to the length of the programme and the amount of contact involved. The coaching programmes that we provide generally run for three months (14 weeks) with two sessions per week. However, a great deal of flexibility is possible. You can request anything from the standard 14-week, twice a week programme to a programme in which you decide on a session-by-session basis whether or not to continue the coaching. When determining the duration and contact frequency, you must consider the following questions:

- What is the nature of the coaching objective? (theme, difficulty level etc.).
- How long can you make the programme? (how soon must the objective be achieved?).
- How busy is the client? (is an accelerated program possible?).
- What is the available budget? (how many coaching hours can be included in the programme?).

As the summary shows, it is important to keep in mind the objective of the programme and how much time you have to achieve it. If somebody wants to realize their coaching objective quickly, then you can choose a short duration with frequent contact. E-coaching makes it possible to schedule a rapid succession of contact moments on a limited budget. However, the client must be able to devote enough time to the programme to have a realistic chance of success.

4. Coaching techniques and tools

The fourth decision relates to coaching methods, tools and techniques. E-coaching is optimally compatible with a wide variety of these tools. In Chapter 5, we explained how coaches from a wide range of disciplines can easily integrate their techniques into the ABC model. There is also myriad of interesting techniques that can be used in e-coaching programmes. Ultimately, everything that is available online can be used in the coaching process provided it makes a positive contribution to achieving the coaching objective. This includes instruments such as 360 degree feedback, tests, questionnaires, card games and written exercises. Some tools that you can apply in F2F coaching require a slight adjustment for use within an e-coaching programme. For example, if you use coaching cards during F2F sessions, they would have to be substituted for digital versions in an e-coaching session. There are also techniques that cannot be digitized, such as coaching with the aid of large equipment or resources (i.e. equine-assisted coaching). These techniques can therefore only be combined with e-coaching as part of a hybrid program, in which both online and F2F sessions are conducted.

Once you have determined the type of coaching, chosen the most suitable medium of communication, established the contact frequency and duration of the programme and selected the right tools, instruments and techniques, your e-coaching programme is almost ready for use.

11.3 Deciding what to charge

In the previous paragraph, we discussed how to design an e-coaching programme. However, one key factor that was not mentioned is the price (both cost price and sale price). We would like to devote specific attention to this factor, as it is the subject of a huge number of questions, assumptions and misconceptions from coaches and clients alike. Clients in particular believe that e-coaching will be much cheaper than F2F coaching, while this is only partly true. Savings are certainly made on traveling time and costs, but the number of coaching hours and related expenses remains more or less the same. The following is a list of the costs involved with e-coaching:

- Overheads (general business expenses).
- Technology costs (software licenses, Internet, equipment).
- Cost of coaching resources (questionnaires, instruments, tools etc.).
- Coaching fees (hourly rate).

The overhead costs of e-coaching are relatively low as the coach doesn't have to rent or buy any office space to conduct the sessions. Travelling time/costs and representation costs (i.e. appropriate clothing) are not required. However, e-coaches do incur other expenses, such as software licenses (free software may be available, although we don't recommend this due to security and privacy risks – see Chapter 10). There is also a third cost category that applies to both F2F coaches and e-coaches: the cost of coaching resources. Finally, the most significant expense is the time that the coach invests in the coaching programme.

11.3.1 Appraising the value of your service

To maintain a viable business, you must ensure that your income covers all of the costs involved in running your e-coaching programmes. Furthermore, unless you are operating in the non-profit sector, you must ensure that your income is significantly higher than your costs. There are two ways to determine your rates. One way is to make a list of all your costs and work out how much money you need to make ends meet. The other way is to establish the value of your services and base your rates on this. If you use the second method, then it is important to remember that the value of your services doesn't necessarily increase if you start e-coaching. Coaching is still the core service, no matter what medium is used to provide it. Depending on your own profit objectives, you may decide to offer a discount for e-coaching in comparison to your F2F coaching. This reflects the reduced overheads that you will incur. However, if you believe that your services are not intrinsically different once you start e-coaching, then you may choose not to offer a discount.

11.3.2 Determining your hourly rate

Most coaches charge an hourly rate for the coaching they provide. This hourly rate usually includes all overheads. Sometimes additional costs are charged for questionnaires, tests etc. The hourly rate can differ significantly between coaches. According to results of the 2012 ICF Global Coaching Study the average hourly rate among independent coaches is around US$200 per hour. The rates for registered coaches roughly depended on their level of experience and their certification. Coaches who belong to a professional association charge around US$240. The coach's background and target market also influence the hourly rate. For example, a Master Practitioner (the highest EMCC level) and Master Certified Coach (the highest ICF level) tend to offer higher rates. E-coach also tends to charge on an hourly basis. How much to charge per hour is entirely up to you.

When conducting telephone, video and chat coaching, it is easy to record how many hours you have worked and charge accordingly. Clients can also easily keep track of this. However, this is not possible for e-mail coaching. Clients cannot accurately determine how long it takes you to write your messages. Even for coaches, this can be difficult to estimate correctly. For this reason, based on our own experience and that of many other e-coaches, we have calculated an average duration of *20 minutes* per written message. This is the average time it takes an experienced e-coach to write a message using the eCP method.

11.3.3 Determining a programme fee

In general, programme fees are determined by the number of hours worked by the coach multiplied by the coach's hourly rate. In this situation, all of the coach's costs are included in the hourly rate. By calculating the average duration per session (i.e.

writing a single message), you can use a formula to calculate the fee for a coaching program. This formula is as follows:

$$Hr \frac{Dx \times Fx \times 20}{60} = \text{programme fee}$$

Key:

Hr = the coach's hourly rate

Dx = the duration of the program in days (d), weeks (w) or months (m)

Fx = the contact frequency in days (d), weeks (w) or months (m)

20 = average time per contact moment (in minutes)

60 = one hour expressed in minutes

FIGURE 11.1 Formula fee-calculation e-coaching

The above formula enables you to determine how much to charge per hour. You can also use it to calculate the overall effect if the parameters are changed. It is therefore easy to work out what would happen to the programme fee if the contact frequency was reduced or the duration of the coaching programme was shortened.

Example calculation

Assume your client wants to arrange a course to boost their leadership skills. The main focus is the improvement of listening skills. You agree to a 12-week programme with 2 e-mail sessions per week (i.e. the coach will respond twice a week). For executive coaching, we charge US$250 per hour, exclusive of VAT. All overheads are included in this hourly rate. The programme fee is therefore calculated as follows:

$$250 \times \frac{12 \times 2 \times 20}{60} = 2.000$$

The overall program fee is $2,000 USD (exclusive of VAT)

FIGURE 11.2 Example fee-calculation e-coaching

The overall program fee is $2,000 USD (exclusive of VAT)

Another way to determine the programme fee is to base it on the client's budget. In this case, you would enter the overall total and your hourly rate into the formula. You can then experiment with the contact frequency and programme duration. You can also do this to calculate the cost of a hybrid programme by entering the number of online contact moments and the number of F2F hours. The formula with then give the overall fee for the hybrid programme. A final example is a 'coaching credit card' model. With this model, clients buy a card with a certain number of credits on it (5, 10, 20 etc.) Upon purchase, each card is valid for a certain period of time. Each credit is worth one session, and the price of the card is based on the coach's hourly rate. Clients can then use these credits within the validity period to schedule sessions with the coach.

NB: For every calculation, the quality of the e-coaching programme is the central focus. In other words, the overall fee depends on exactly what the program requires (see the previous subsection). You must therefore first determine how many sessions will be necessary in order to maximize the programme's chances of success. If the budget proves insufficient to these needs, then it is best to cancel the programme.

11.3.4 Extra investment (time/money)

In the formula for calculating the overall fee for an e-coaching programme, we assume that on average, it takes 20 minutes to write an e-mail. This average is based on the time it takes experienced e-coaches to write a message using the eCP method. For coaches who are just getting started with e-coaching, this is not a realistic average. Beginner e-coaches usually need between 40–60 minutes to write effective messages. You must therefore allow for this when getting started with e-coaching. It is not advisable to increase your fees to offset this extra time, as you run the risk of pricing yourself out of the market. You must therefore invest the extra time for free while honing your skills as an e-coach. The more you practice and build up your experience, the less time it will take to write the e-mails. You can speed up this process by investing in effective training, e.g. by taking an e-coach training course or by hiring a supervisor to assist you during your first e-coaching programmes.

11.4 The e-coaching agreement

Every coaching programme is based on a coaching agreement. This agreement contains all of the professional agreements between coach and client. To a great extent, e-coaching agreements are the same as regular coaching agreements. The definitive agreement is drawn up in consultation with the client. In this section, we provide a checklist containing the 12 essential factors of e-coaching agreements. This checklist is based on the experiences of the e-coaches we work with, as well as an example agreement made available by the EMCC. For a detailed example agreement, see the text box 'Spotlight: Example of an e-coaching agreement for a full online coaching programme'.

Checklist for setting up an e-coaching agreement:

1   *Client:* State the name and address of the client. If the agreement is made via the client's company, then the details of the company must also be included as well as an official representative of the company. Also include your own business details.

2   *Objective:* Record the objective of the coaching programme. You can also include the client's motivation and any possible subgoals. If you are using the ABC model, then it is advisable to formulate preliminary objectives here and then work them out in greater detail during the first stage (Analyse). In this

case, provisional objectives would be recorded in the agreement.

3   *Duration:* Note down the duration of the program in days, weeks or months.

4   *Frequency and type of sessions:* State the number of sessions and categorize them according to the communication medium used. For example, 2 x 1.5 hour F2F sessions + 9 e-mails + 10 text messages. Also state when the sessions will take place during the course of the programme. If cancellation terms apply (e.g. for F2F sessions), then record the terms under which this is permitted (for both coach and client) and whether costs are due in the event of a cancellation.

5   *Invoicing:* Record the fee for the coaching. This can be a fee for the entire programme or separate invoices after a set number of sessions (see previous paragraph). State when the payment must be made. Usually, shorter e-coaching programmes are paid for in advance while payment in instalments is more customary for longer programmes. An example of a typical instalment plan is that the fee is paid via three invoices, one prior to the start of the programme, one halfway through the program and one upon completion of the programme. If you choose this option, then remember to note down the payment term (e.g. payment within 14 days of the invoice date).

6   *Use of materials and tools:* If known, record which materials and tools will be used during the programme and whether a surcharge applies. Clearly indicate who holds the intellectual property rights for these resources and whether the client is permitted to use these tools outside and/or following completion of the coaching programme.

7   *Use of online communication resources:* Write down which communication devices will be used during the programme. Record who owns these devices, how the data will be sent, who has access to the data, how the data is stored and secured, and how long the data will be stored for.

8   *Best endeavours obligation:* Record the mutual obligations that apply during the programme. Naturally, the coach has a number of obligations, but it is also advisable to state what is expected of the client. By recording this in black and white, you can refer back to it during the process. The obligations are categorized as follows:

- *Coach:* The coach will make the best possible effort to provide professionally competent supervision and support during the client's development. The coach will strive to respond to messages from the client within the agreed time period (see also Section 11.5: Expectation management)

- *Client:* The client will devote sufficient time, actively participate in the process and maintain an open-minded attitude in order to ensure that the programme has a realistic chance of success. The client is obliged to complete the assignments set by the coach to the best of their ability both during and outside the sessions. The client must also complete these assignments in accordance with the instructions given by the coach. The client will strive to fulfil the agreed contact frequency.

9   *Evaluation:* Record how and when the programme will be evaluated. Also

include the medium via which the evaluation will be conducted (e.g. online or during a final F2F meeting) and what the evaluation will focus on. If the coaching was commissioned by someone other than the client (e.g. the client's employer), then state with whom the evaluation will be conducted.

10   *Code of conduct and complaints procedure:* Record here whether a particular code of conduct applies to the programme. If applicable, refer to the code of conduct in the agreement and add the full code in the appendix. If no code of conduct is applicable, then record at least how the client's privacy is protected. Also state where clients can report any complaints they may have. See also Section 11.5: Expectation management.

11   *Resolutory conditions:* Record the conditions under which the coach, coachee and client can dissolve the agreement. If general terms and conditions apply to your practice, then refer to them in the agreement and add them in the appendix.

12   *Signature:* Ensure that both you and the client sign the agreement. If a party other than the coachee commissioned the coaching programme and/or is responsible for payment, then make sure that this party also signs the agreement.

Spotlight: Example of an e-coaching agreement for a full online coaching programme

COACHING CONTRACT*

Client
Name
Address
Postcode
Telephone number

Invoice address

Coach
Name of coach
Name of business
Business address
Postcode
Ch. of Comm. no.

You hereby hire me as your coach, as you wish to {add draft objective}. Change takes time. As a result, we will conduct an e-coaching programme with a duration of {x} weeks. During these {x} weeks, our communication will be conducted as much as possible via the digital coaching environment

Pluform.com. This will facilitate effective coaching and help prevent misunderstandings.

Contact frequency

The type of e-coaching selected for this programme is e-mail coaching. We will contact each other at least {x} times per week via Pluform. You can expect a response to your messages within {x} working days. I also expect you to respond to my messages within {x} working days (this includes possible requests for extra time to complete an assignment). Once the {x}-week programme is completed, then we can, if desired, extend the programme on a week-to-week basis.

Confidentiality

Everything that we communicate to each other during the programme, whether verbally or in writing, will be held in the strictest confidence, unless doing so would constitute a criminal act.

Pluform.com is a secure working environment. You will be granted access via a password that you will determine yourself, and the communication conducted between us will not be read by any third parties without your consent. Everything that you save in your Pluform client profile will be accessible to you for at least three months following completion of the coaching programme, unless you decide to delete it before this period has elapsed.

Coach–client relationship

During the coaching programme, we will work together to realize your coaching objective. That means that the goals, resources and choices of you, the client take priority over those of myself, the coach.

What you can expect from me is that I will share my knowledge and experience in order to support you during the development process. What I expect from you is that you will maintain an open mind regarding the coaching programme and make the effort required to succeed. I take for granted that you know what is best for you and that you are capable of making decisions for yourself based on your own initiative and insights. As a result, you are also responsible for the choices you make and you are personally liable for your own behaviour. If my coaching does not meet your expectations, let me know. In such an event, I will do my utmost to adjust the coach–client relationship to your satisfaction.

Payment

The fee for the {x}-week coaching programme is {x} USD (exclusive of VAT) and will be paid in {x} instalments of {x} USD (exclusive of VAT). Payment must be made within 14 days of the invoice date.

Cancellation and costs

In the event that termination of the programme is desired before the completion of the agreed {x}-week programme, then both parties must observe a notice period of {x} days. In such cases, if payment has already been made, then the amount paid for the remainder of the coaching programme (once the {x}-day notice period has elapsed) will be refunded.

If you are unable to participate in the Pluform activities during the {x}-week period due to illness or vacation, please let me know. If desired, a one-off extension of one week can be added free of charge to the end of the {x}-week period to make up for the missed week.

NB: If you are inactive on Pluform for one week without notifying me beforehand, then the complimentary extension does not apply.

Evaluation

Upon completion of the coaching programme, you will receive a digital evaluation form with which you can assess the coaching programme and my performance.

Codes of conduct and complaints procedure

My General Terms and Conditions apply to this coaching agreement (see appendix).

Signatures

Client's name _____   Date _____

Coach's name _____   Date _____

* Disclaimer: No rights can be derived in any way from this example.

11.5 Expectation management

In the last section, we presented a checklist for drawing up e-coaching agreements. Coaching agreements ensure that both coach and client know what they can expect from each other. The agreement mainly addresses professional expectations, as the more implicit and unspoken expectations are difficult to get down on paper. However, they still play a role in the coaching process. Due to the nature of e-coaching (i.e. little or no F2F contact), it is difficult to get a handle on these subtler expectations. It is therefore important to make agreements in advance about as many specific expectations as possible. In the following subsections, we will discuss a number of frequently occurring problems regarding implicit expectations on the part of both coach and client.

11.5.1 Expectations regarding availability

As e-coaching theoretically makes the coach available 24 hours a day, 7 days a week, some clients expect you to be available whenever they wish. It is therefore advisable to agree when you are available to give coaching and within what time period you will respond to messages from the client. It is important for the client to know when they can expect a response to their message. Some coaches pledge to respond within 24 hours (on working days), some designate a particular day of the week for writing messages and some designate days on which they will not respond (e.g. 'Monday and Thursday are my days off'). These are just a few examples, and numerous other arrangements are possible. What you agree with the client depends entirely on your personal schedule and the design of the coaching programme.

Determining when to respond to your clients' messages helps give your working week structure. Beginner e-coaches in particular have the tendency to spend all their time working on and thinking about their coaching. It is all too easy to end up almost obsessing about a client's message. Reading a message last thing on Friday can result in the message bouncing around your brain all weekend. The most important piece of advice in this regard is 'know yourself'. If you find it easy to detach yourself from your work outside office hours, then it is less risky to read messages late in the day. Proper management of your own time and expectations is therefore equally as important as the client's.

11.5.2 Expectations about accelerated coaching

E-coaching greatly facilitates accelerated programmes. This acceleration can be achieved by planning small, targeted action steps in an environment that is relevant to the client, and providing a great deal of positive reinforcement and support when the client needs it (see also the ABC model and the eCP method). This approach can lead to the client expecting rapid progress from the very start. This is usually not the case, which can cause disappointment. In reality, true acceleration is not immediately possible in the first stage (Analyse). With e-coaching, more time is needed in the analysis stage than with F2F coaching. This is because the first stage involves both the crystallization of the coaching objective and the development of the coach–client relationship, and both of these take longer in e-coaching. The real acceleration only begins in stage 2 of the coaching programme (Internalize). During this stage, the client works on achieving their objectives, taking small steps to realize concrete results. Another precondition for this stage is that frequent communication is required. If the coach and client only maintain sporadic contact, then little to no acceleration is possible. It is the coach's job to clarify when, where and under what circumstances acceleration will take place during the coaching process. If a programme features only a limited number of sessions and/or infrequent contact, then it will be difficult to realize true, lasting behavioural change. This factor must be kept in mind when designing the coaching programme and managing expectations.

11.5.3 Ethical expectations

Clients tend to take it for granted that coaches work in accordance with a professional code of conduct. As a result, this factor is usually overlooked when the client is looking for a coach. Generally, clients only conduct this kind of investigation at a later stage or if problems occur. This is when they will scrutinize whether you are part of an official coaching association and/or whether you are bound by a professional and/or ethical code of conduct. In order to avoid problems or false expectations, it is advisable to explain to the client at an early stage how you deal with ethical matters such as privacy, coach–client confidentiality, data storage, complaints procedures etc.

The easiest way to give your client peace of mind about your professional ethics and practice is to join a professional association like the International Coaching Federation (ICF), European Mentoring and Coaching Council (EMCC) or other local branch. You can then provide the client with the association's code of conduct in the appendix of the coaching agreement. However, this doesn't cover absolutely everything, as the codes of conduct of these associations have not yet been specifically adapted to accommodate e-coaching. For example, the following is written in the EMCC Code of Ethics and the ICG Code of Ethics:

- *Section 4. The coach/mentor will:*
  Disclose information only where explicitly agreed with the client and sponsor (where one exists), unless the coach/mentor believes that there is convincing evidence of serious danger to the client or others if the information is withheld.... (EMCC Code of Ethics, 2014):
- *Section 1.7. I will maintain, store, and dispose of any records created during my coaching business in a manner that promotes confidentiality, security and privacy, and complies with any applicable laws and agreements (ICF Code of Ethics, 2014)*

In practice, both provisions are relatively simple to ensure for traditional coaches, as this simply requires them to refrain from talking to third parties about the information and to keep the conversation records under lock and key. However, this is more complicated when applied to online coaching practice. Consider e-mail, chat, video and telephone coaching: do you really know how safe the client's data is? What happens to the messages sent to the client over the Internet? Who can view them and where are they stored? Many coaches use their client's e-mail applications and/or free applications such as Outlook and Gmail. As a result, all messages are saved within the network of the client's company and/or on the foreign servers belonging to the providers of the free applications in question. In such situations, it is difficult to trace what happens to the e-correspondence. By using these applications, you may be unwittingly violating the confidentiality provision described above. You are therefore ethically bound to use communication solutions that minimize the likelihood of breaching the client's confidentiality. If, for whatever reason, this is not possible, then you must inform the client of this matter. Clients can then decide for themselves whether they want to conduct the coaching programme in this way. See also Section 10.2: Prerequisites for a digital coaching environment.

Nowadays, developments in the field of online coaching are coming thick and fast. It is therefore only a matter of time before professional associations adjust their codes of conduct and ethics to encompass online coaching. One organization that has already done so is the *Association for Counselling and Therapy Online* (ACTO). This code can therefore serve as inspiration for current and future e-coaches.

11.6 Summary

Organizing e-coaching programmes is about more than just having the right coaching skills and expertise. This chapter summarized all important preconditions for successful programmes. Once of the major factors is the design of the programme. You can offer programmes that are entirely online or you can organize hybrid programmes that combine both F2F and e-coaching. Another essential precondition is setting the right fee, i.e. calculating the costs incurred and the sale price of your services. We explained which costs have to be accounted for and we gave a handy formula for calculating a suitable fee for your coaching programmes. A coaching agreement is the cornerstone of both F2F and e-coaching programmes. To a great extent, e-coaching agreements contain similar elements to F2F coaching agreements. Based on a handy checklist, we summarized all of the essential aspects required for an e-coaching agreement. At the end of the chapter, we addressed expectation management from the perspective of both coach and client. For example, many clients assume that e-coaching makes coaches available to them 24/7. In order to ensure realistic expectations, you must make concrete agreements regarding availability and contactability.

In the final part of the book, the insights from Parts I and II will be brought to life by means of a detailed description of an entire e-coaching programme, including all of the communication exchanged between the coach and client. Throughout this programme description, we will highlight all of the stages and steps that the coach followed in accordance with the ABC model and the eCP method.

PART III
Detailed e-coaching programme

In the final part of the book, we provide an example of a complete e-coaching programme conducted by e-coach Marcel Herwegh, who has been fully trained in the use of the ABC model and the eCP method, and Peter Young, a client who has never completed a coaching programme before. Although every programme is unique and there is no single correct way to give coaching, it can still be helpful to have an example of how a successful coaching programme could look. This example is therefore only intended to provide ideas and inspiration, not to tell you how to do your job. The programme was conducted in the online coaching environment Pluform.com. All of the communication between Marcel and Peter can be found in this environment. This includes all of the messages from the dialogue, all internal e-mails, all of the documents that Marcel uses and all of the assignments completed by Peter. Throughout this example programme, we will highlight the specific steps and stages of the ABC model, as well as explain the linguistic strategies used by the coach. This example programme helps bring to life the concept of e-coaching by means of the ABC model, eCP method and Pluform platform.

Introduction

Peter Young learned about the concept of e-coaching via his company's HR department. They are planning an employee satisfaction survey, and Peter knows his score won't be anything to write home about. He therefore decides to get some help and work on this aspect. The prospect of an e-coaching programme is attractive to him as it allows him to structure the coaching around his busy schedule, enabling him to respond when he has the time. After exploring the eCoachPro network, he selected Marcel Herwegh as his coach.

Peter sent Marcel a brief e-mail explaining that he was looking for an e-coach for a two-month period and asking about Marcel's availability. Marcel responded that he was indeed available and keen to arrange a collaboration. Marcel then created an Pluform client profile for Peter and sent an internal e-mail via Pluform that briefly explained how the coaching environment works. Furthermore, a coaching agreement was drawn up and signed by both Marcel and Peter. The invoice for the coaching fee was also included in this internal e-mail as an attachment, and as soon as proof of payment was provided, the coaching programme commenced.

Example coaching programme

Session 1, week 1 – dialogue window

Dear Peter,

It is my pleasure to welcome you to the online coaching environment Pluform.

Our e-coaching program begins today. I look forward to working with you over the next eight weeks!

I suggest we use the first couple of days of the program to get to know each other better. Therfore I would like you to tell me something about yourself and explain what motivated you to take this coaching program.

I look forward to your response and I wish you good luck with the program!

Yours sincerely,
Marcel Herwegh

(ABC model: Analyze stage – explore)

Session 2, week 1 – dialogue window

Dear Marcel,

I'm a middle manager, aged 36. After completing a degree in econometrics, I quickly forged a career in the financial world. I currently supervise a team of 41 professionals. I work at the Drost & Co. Bank, providing loans to large organizations. I enjoy my job, but I sometimes find it difficult to maintain relationships with clients and employees. The bank has recently adjusted our pay system to include employee satisfaction as a factor in determining wages. So I really need to work on this.

Yours sincerely,
Peter Young

Explanation: here, the client says '...I really need to work on this'. This is an assertive – the client is trying to convince the coach. The coach will therefore react to this assertive in his response.

Session 3, week 1 – dialogue window

Dear Peter,

Wow, that was a quick reaction! A good start is half the battle, so I'm glad to see that you're motivated to make a change. Thank you for the insight into your career. I think it's a very smart move on your part to use your company's changing pay structure as a catalyst for personal and professional development.

Before we get started, let me tell you something about myself. I am 41 years old and I have over 10 years' experience in the business sector as a manager, coach and trainer. For the last four years, I have been working for eCoachPro as an executive coach. I mainly specialize in career development and personal leadership. I am a certified e-coach and an Associate certified Coach with the International Coach Federation. Many of my coaching programs are conducted via Pluform. I look forward to working with you!

In the assignment section I have provided some practical information about the coaching program and how we will maintain contact. If you are unclear about anything, feel free to ask for an explanation.

Let me know if you accept the work agreements. Once these are agreed, we can make a start!

Yours sincerely,
Marcel

(ABC model: Analyze stage – explore)

Explanation: here, the coach gives a compliment at the start of the message to acknowledge the assertive used by the client in his message. The client must be acknowledged and/or complimented in every message.

By closing the message in this way, the coach is inviting the client to respond, which activates the client. This is important as it helps give the coaching process more impetus. Every message must have an activating closing sentence that conveys an expectation.

Session 3, week 1 – assignment window

Dear Peter,

We are just about ready to get started with your coaching program. In order to ensure an effective collaboration, I have drawn up an e-coaching agreement. I would like to ask you to read it through carefully, print it out, sign it and upload the signed copy to the Pluform library.

Explanation: clear and unambiguous agreements for the coaching ensure the program is built on firm foundations. It is important that mutual expectations are clearly established and understood.

COACHING AGREEMENT

Client
Peter Young
Drost & Co Bank
15 Example Avenue
MA 02115
Boston, Massachusetts
USA
+1 555-267-5555

06-05555555
Invoice address is the same as the above address

Coach
Marcel Herwegh
eCoachPro
Willem II Straat 19
5038 BW Tilburg
The Netherlands
Ch. of Comm. no: 55050727

You hereby hire me as your coach, as you wish to improve your managerial skills. Change takes time. As a result, we will conduct an e-coaching program with a duration of 9 weeks. During these 9 weeks, our communication will be conducted as much as possible via the digital coaching environment Pluform.com. This will facilitate effective coaching and help prevent misunderstandings.

Contact frequency
The type of e-coaching selected for this program is e-mail coaching. We will contact each other at least twice a week via Pluform.com. You can expect a response to your messages within 2 days, including at the weekend. I don't expect you to respond to my messages at the weekend, but I do want you to respond to my messages within 2 working days (this includes possible requests for extra time to complete an assignment). Once the 9-week program is completed, we can, if desired, extend the program on a week-to-week basis.

Confidentiality

All that we communicate during the program, whether verbally or in writing, will be kept strictly confidential by me, providing it is not conflicting with the law.

Pluform.com is a secure working environment. You will be granted access via a password that you will determine yourself, and the communication conducted between us will not be read by any third parties without your consent. Everything that you save in your Pluform client profile will be accessible to you for at least three months following completion of the coaching program, unless you decide to delete it before this period has elapsed.

Coach–client relationship

During the coaching program, we will work together to realize your coaching objective. That means that the goals, resources and choices of you, the client, take priority over those of myself, the coach.

What you can expect from me is that I will share my knowledge and experience in order to support you during the development process. What I expect from you is that you will maintain an open mind regarding the coaching program and make the effort required to succeed. I consider that you know what is best for you and that you are capable of making decisions for yourself based on your own initiative and insights. As a result, you are responsible for the choices you make and accountable for your own behaviour. If my coaching does not meet your expectations, let me know. In such an event, I will do my utmost to adjust the coach–client relationship to your satisfaction.

Payment

The fee for the 9-week coaching program is $1.500 USD (exclusive of VAT) and will be paid in 3 instalments of $500 USD (exclusive of VAT). The first invoice will be sent in week 1, the second in week 5, and the third upon completion of the coaching program. Payment must be made within 14 days of the invoice date.

Cancellation and costs

In the event that termination of the program is desired before the completion of the agreed 9-week program, then both parties must observe a notice period of 7 days. In such cases, if payment has already been made, then the amount paid for the remainder of the coaching program (once the 7-day notice period has elapsed) will be refunded.

If you are unable to participate in the Pluform activities during the 9-week period due to illness or vacation, please let me know. If desired, a one-off extension of one week can be added free of charge to the end of the 9-week period to make up for the missed week.

NB: If you are inactive on Pluform for one week without notifying me beforehand, then the complimentary extension does not apply.

Evaluation
Upon completion of the coaching program, you will receive a digital evaluation form with which you can assess the coaching program and my performance.

Codes of conduct and complaints procedure
The Code of Ethics of the International Coaching Federation (ICF) is applicable to this coaching agreement (see appendix).
Signatures

Peter Young _____   Date _____

Marcel Herwegh _____   Date _____

If you have any questions or comments about the above coaching agreement, then feel free to contact me.

Yours sincerely,
Marcel

Session 4, week 2 – dialogue window

Dear Marcel,

I've read the agreement through carefully and I agree to it wholeheartedly. I've signed it and uploaded it to the Pluform library.

I'll sometimes be able to respond at weekends too, as I often work through my e-mails then.

I look forward to the taking the next step!

Yours,
Peter

Explanation: the client expresses an expectation he has for the coach.

Session 5, week 2 – dialogue window

Dear Peter,

You're really getting to grips with Pluform! Thanks for your quick response and for signing the agreement. Now we can really get started!

You mention that you have difficulty maintaining relationships with your clients and employees. I'd like us to investigate the root cause of this problem, so I've set up an exercise. You can find it in the assignments section.

Please complete the exercise in your worksheet section.

Yours,
Marcel

(ABC model: Analyse stage – explore)

Explanation: this message includes examples of various linguistic strategies. The message is written as concisely as possible and uses positive relationship-oriented measures. A compliment is given (strategy 15) and the coach confirms that the coaching program has definitely begun (strategy 12). This answers the expectations expressed by the client in his message.

The coach initiates the analysis stage by setting exploratory assignments aimed at increasing awareness.

Session 6, week 2 – dialogue window

Dear Marcel,

I've written my answers to your exercise in the worksheet section.

I await your reaction with interest.

Yours,
Peter

Session 6, week 2 – worksheet window

What makes the relationships with my employees difficult is that I often feel that we are not on the same page. People often seem to focus on subjects that I don't think are relevant to our work. I then try to explain why other things have to take priority, but they generally don't listen. This creates friction because I start to lose patience with the inefficiency of their methods. I also find it difficult to talk to people who are very emotional.

I find contact with clients difficult as they always want more from us, which we frequently can't give them. We're under such close scrutiny from the Financial Markets Authority and we have to stick to the rules. Many clients find this difficult to accept and constantly moan.

Session 7, week 2 – dialogue window

Dear Peter,

Thank you for your detailed description of the problem – it is very helpful. From your account, I derive that you are a man of action and you seem to feel the behaviour of some of your employees and clients frequently hinders you from taking your desired course of action. Am I right?

Over the next couple of weeks, let's specifically focus on the relationship with your employees. Focusing on one particular target group will help make the program simpler. We can then take the necessary steps to deal with the matter at hand: boosting employee satisfaction.

To get started on this matter, you can find an exercise in the assignments section.

Good luck, and I'll speak to you in a couple of days.

Yours,
Marcel

(ABC model: Analyse stage – reality)

Session 7, week 2 – assignment window

Describe a conversation with an employee that you think went badly.

What was the situation?
Who was involved?
What was the aim of the conversation?
What did you say?
How did the person react?
What did you think and feel? (Happy, angry, impatient etc.)
What was the result of the conversation?

Describe the event in the first person and in the present tense.

Explanation: this is still stage 1 of the ABC model: Analysis. The coach asks the client to describe his current situation in detail.

Session 8, week 3 – dialogue window

Dear Marcel,

Yes, that's a very accurate description of me and my situation.

You asked me to give an example of a conversation that went badly. Unfortunately I didn't have to think back very far to find one. You can read my description of it in the assignments section.

I look forward to your response.

Kind regards,
Peter

Session 8, week 3 – worksheet window

It is Friday morning and I am talking to one of my employees. I had asked him to draw up a agreement for an important deal that I will be negotiating on Monday. This assignment was set for him on Wednesday. He said that he didn't have enough information to make the desired changes to the client's agreement. I gave him the client's information, including prognoses, and told him that this would be enough. He kept saying that he doesn't know how to draw up customized agreements and that he needs more time to do it. I say that he should get a similar agreement from a co-worker and base the customized agreement on that. He says 'It's just not as simple as...', but doesn't finish his sentence. I say that it is that simple and tell him to get that specific agreement from his co-worker. He turns around and says nothing. I get impatient as nothing is happening. I tell him that it'll be fine and he can ask his co-worker to help if he has any trouble. I ask him to print out the agreement and have it on my desk by the end of the afternoon so I can take it with me on Monday. He walks out of the door without saying anything, but lets out a deep sigh. It irritates me that he is being so childish and not taking what is clearly the obvious course of action for this task.

Session 9, week 3 – dialogue window

Dear Peter,

Your description is very clear and vivid. It therefore gives me good insight into the difficulty you have in your interpersonal contact. Repetition, procrastination, impatience, sighing, irritation – I can understand why you want to make a change.

To start off, let's look more closely at this conversation and what is going through your head. In the library section, you can find some information about communication, and a related assignment is waiting for you in the assignments section.

The assignment is quite a big one, so take the time you need. If you have any questions along the way, feel free to send me an e-mail via the internal e-mail system.

Kind regards,
Marcel

(ABC model: Analyse stage – reality)

Explanation: here, the coach makes use of linguistic strategy 7: Assume/offer/confirm a common perspective. The client is boosted by the coach's acknowledgement.

With large assignments, it is good to let the client know that they can take longer to complete it than the agreed reaction time. This prevents the client from feeling pressured. If the reaction is not sent on time, you can send a text message to ask if the client is having difficulty with the assignment.

Session 9, week 3 – assignment window

Read through the conversation in the document. The right-hand column is the actual conversation, while the left-hand column represents your thought processes during the conversation. Now examine at the conversation with your employee that you wrote about. What unspoken thoughts appeared in your left-hand column?

Explanation: the ABC model also provides opportunities for knowledge transfer, where the coach shares information with the client.

Session 9, week 3 – library window

Explanation: documents containing theory or articles can be placed in the library section for reference.

Two-column communication
(based on the work of Chris Argyris and Donald A. Schön)

People are constantly communicating. They want to convey knowledge, gain new information, express emotions, forge relationships, and co-operate effectively. Saying nothing can also be a form of communication.

When people communicate, many different things happen at once. If you observe a conversation between two people, they both have their own thoughts, feelings and intentions. These are not always expressed, but they always influence the words that are is said and the actions that are visible to the other person.

When communicating with another person, as well as hearing what is said out loud, you can also register things that are not said. Non-verbal behaviour is a major part of this, as is the intonation used by the person you are talking to. Both factors convey information about the possible intentions behind what is verbalized.

As long as the other person does not express their thoughts, feelings or intentions out loud, all you can do is make assumptions about the nature or content of the unspoken information. Generally, these assumptions provoke thoughts and emotions in your mind in response to these (assumed) intentions. Communication can be separated into two columns. The right-hand column documents the actual words that were communicated (verbally or in writing), and the left-hand column represents your unspoken thoughts and feelings.

An example of a two–column conversation:

Martin's thoughts and feelings	What was said
Hello? Do I look like your secretary? You're the one who wanted to reach out to a new target group. Why should I be lumbered with extra work?	Joan: Have you spoken to David? You sent him a new mailing list, but it was incomplete. He wants you to give him the extra information so he can send the mailing as soon as the program is ready.
All she ever does is make a fuss. Why can't she do something herself for once?	Martin: I haven't got time to do that this week. I've got several urgent assignments that need to be completed by the weekend.
	Joan: Look, at this rate the mailing is only going to reach half of the managers who need it. We'll then be messing about for ages trying to get it to everyone else. And not only that, it ruins the simultaneity if everybody doesn't get it at once.
That's his job, not mine.	Martin: Well ask Bernard to complete the list. He's the one responsible for program support.
For God's sake!! I just told you I'm snowed under with work?	Joan: He won't be back at work until Friday, and the mailing needs to be sent by then. I want you to do it this afternoon.
	Martin: I don't have time. Why not send the e-mail in two weeks when everyone's back from their holidays? Half of the managers aren't here so they won't get the messages at the same time anyway.
Now she tells me. Well, I guess there's no getting out of this one.	Joan: The board want the mailing sent this week.
	Martin: I'll make sure David gets the complete list before noon tomorrow.
	Joan: Ok, agreed.

The whole process in the left-hand column often remains unspoken. Both parties hide not only their left-hand columns, but also the assumptions they make about the other person's left-hand column. This influences the way they act. To make conversations more productive, it helps to express as much of your left-hand column as possible. However, people often look for 'good reasons' to avoid saying what they think. It is therefore advisable to carefully examine these reasons.

Session 10, week 3 – dialogue window

Hello Marcel,

That was an interesting assignment! I have always been aware of the fact that other people often don't say everything they think, but I've never really realized that I also have so many thoughts that remain unsaid. Now I know they exist, I keep hearing left-hand columns everywhere!)

I'm quite shocked by my own reactions. Now I see what I said in writing, I can see that I was very abrupt and irritable. I'm starting to realize why my interpersonal relationships don't run very smoothly...

Regards,
Peter

Explanation: here, the client reveals how he felt via an expressive. The coach will acknowledge this expressive in his response.

Session 10, week 3 – worksheet window

O = Original
LHC = Left-hand column

O: **He says he doesn't have enough information to make the necessary changes to the client's agreement.**

LHC: Oh, here we go again. Why do you always make such a fuss? You're paid a lot of money to do your job. So do it!

O: **He keeps saying that he doesn't know how to draw up a customized agreement and that he'll need more time to do it.**

LHC: It's always something with you, isn't it? You could easily do this in two days. Why can't you try harder?

O: **I say that he should get a similar agreement from a co-worker and base the customized agreement on that. He says 'It's just not as simple as...', but doesn't finish his sentence.**

LHC: It is as simple as that. Now shut up and get on with it, I've got work to do.

O: **I say that it is that simple and tell him to get that specific agreement from his co-worker. He turns around and says nothing.**

LHC: What are you doing just standing there? Do it so I can get on with my work.

O: **I get impatient as nothing is happening. I tell him that it'll be fine and he can ask his co-worker to help if he has any trouble.**

LHC: Ok, problem solved, right?

O: **I ask him to print out the agreement and have it on my desk by the end of the afternoon so I can take it with me on Monday. He walks out of the door without saying anything, but lets out a deep sigh.**

LHC: Loser! Now I'm annoyed again. Grr!

Session 11, week 3 – dialogue window

Hello Peter,

You certainly got to grips with the assignment – well done! What a clever idea to separate the two in the conversation. Even though it can be difficult sometimes, it really does help to examine your own left-hand column, doesn't it? The irritation you feel certainly affects the way the conversation plays out.

You say you're starting to understand why your contact with others often goes badly. That's great – awareness is key to making a change. Before we examine what could be done differently, I'd like you to take another look at how you do things. I've set you another assignment that will help you do this.

I look forward to reading it!

Regards,
Marcel

(ABC model: Analyse stage – opportunities)

Explanation: the coach is using linguistic strategy 1: Pay attention to your client. In his message, the client said that he was shocked, so the coach will acknowledge this feeling and show understanding.

Session 11, week 3 – assignment window

Writing out your left-hand column has given you an insight into your contact with others.

What have you learned about your own conduct? In the worksheet section, finish the following sentence:

I'm starting to understand that the problems in my interaction with others **are caused by** ....

The coach is nearing the end of the Analyse stage of the ABC model. He is trying to clearly establish the objective of the coaching program.

Session 12, week 4 – dialogue window

Hello Marcel,

The more I think about it, the more things I remember going wrong. I'm starting to realize just how difficult this is going to be.

I can't wait to hear how we can tackle these issues.

Regards,
Peter

Explanation: once again, the client reveals how he is feeling via an expressive, telling the coach about his desire for collaboration.

Session 12, week 4 – worksheet window

I'm starting to understand that the problems in my interaction with others are caused by... the fact that I am very impatient and I don't think about the needs of others. Because I respond so abruptly, I don't give people a chance to speak. However, I often think that people talk too much, which creates friction and doesn't get us anywhere.

Session 13, week 4 – dialogue window

Hello Peter,

Your assignment shows a great deal of insightful reflection. I think it is very possible that there's a correlation between your own impatience and the needs of others. It's very encouraging to hear that you are motivated to do something about it. We're about to discuss how we will go about changing this behaviour, so this is the perfect moment to pin down exactly what you want to achieve. For this purpose, I've set up an exercise about setting goals and placed it in the assignments section. In the library window, you can find some information that can help you with this exercise.

Let me know exactly what you hope to achieve and we can get right on it!

Regards,
Marcel

(ABC model: Analyse stage – objectives)

Explanation: the coach sidesteps the negative part of the client's message, instead acknowledging the client by paying him a compliment. This shifts the focus back on the positive: starting the journey towards the client's coaching objective.

The coach makes use of linguistic strategy 9: Confirm or assume knowledge of and attentiveness for your client's needs.

The coach uses linguistic strategy 12: Involve both yourself and your client in the activity. He does this by confirming that he is going to work together with the client. This answers the need expressed by the client in his last message.

Session 13, week 4 – assignment window

In the objectives tab (in the 'Edit' section of the right-hand menu), fill in exactly what you want to get out of this coaching program regarding your relationships with employees. In two months, what do you hope will be different?

Formulate goals that are challenging yet achievable, and then give yourself a score for how good you think you currently are at maintaining relationships.

Explanation: the coach helps the client with his assignment by giving him a technique for achieving goals.

Session 13, week 4 – library window

Set inspiring goals

Setting goals seems to be much easier than achieving goals. However, the two are very closely related. A sloppily formulated goal doesn't inspire you to live up to it, while unrealistically high expectations can damage your motivation if you fall short. It often helps to have a carefully selected goal to aim for (whether on paper or in your head), as it gives you a clear understanding of what you want to achieve.

SMART

In the business world, the SMART method is frequently used for setting goals. The letters in this acronym stand for Specific, Measurable, Acceptable, Realistic and Time-bound. Using this method ensures that the goals are clear and achievable. However, are they inspiring?

Key aspects

Naturally, what makes objectives inspiring is the prospect of achieving something you want. How do you increase your chances of success?

- Clearly formulate exactly what you want, e.g. I want to exercise more (rather than I'd like to be less inactive).
- Set goals that relate to issues that you have influence over. Ensure that your behaviour truly contributes to achieving them.
- Be transparent. Ensure that you understand the background of your objectives and the decisive factors in achieving them. You should also share them openly with others.

- Ensure that the objectives are relevant – not only to yourself but to those around you. This increases your chances of success.

Prior achievements

When setting goals, you can also draw inspiration from other successes that you or another person may have had. What worked well? What did it feel like? How can you transfer this success to other situations?

Review

Another way to gain inspiration is to imagine that one year later, you are talking to a good friend and telling them about what you achieved during the coaching program. What are you proud of?

Session 14, week 4 – dialogue window

Hi Marcel!

Thanks for the document.

I certainly have formulated a challenging goal and I am very motivated to achieve this goal.

Based on what I have formulated, I now score no higher than a 5.

That was quite a shock ☹

So, let's start today!

Regards,
Peter

Session 15, week 4 – dialogue window

Hello Peter,

You've set a very clear and sufficiently challenging objective – well done! I can understand that only being able to award yourself 5 out of 10 would come as a shock. Still, I'm impressed by the honesty you showed in order to objectively rate your ability in this way. We now know exactly what we have to work on!

As you may have guessed, there's another assignment waiting for you in the assignments section! :-)

Good luck, and I'll speak to you soon!

Regards,
Marcel

(ABC model: Internalize stage – action)

Explanation: with the objective clearly formulated, the analysis stage of the ABC model is complete. The coach will now begin the second stage: Internalize. In this stage, the client will practice, test and reflect upon new skills. At first the client will do this in theory, then later in a real-life situation.

Session 15, week 4 – assignment window

You have written what occurred in your left-hand column during the conversation with your employee. As we have discussed, people are often quick to assume what is in the other person's left-hand column. Fill in what you think your employee's left-hand column was during this conversation.

Once you have done this, write your reaction in the dialogue window.

Session 16, week 4 – worksheet window

O = Original
YLHC = Your left-hand column
ELHC = Employee's left-hand column

ELHC: Here we go again. He's never going to listen to the fact that I need more time.

O: **He says he doesn't have enough information to make the necessary changes to the client's agreement.**

LHC: Oh, here we go again. Why do you always make such a fuss? You're paid a lot of money to do your job. So do it!

ELHC: Surely he can see that it's difficult to write an agreement like this in such a short time? And what if I get it wrong?

O: **He keeps saying that he can't draw up a custom agreement and that he needs more time.**

LHC: It's always something with you, isn't it? You could easily do this in two days. Why can't you try harder?

O: **I say that he could try basing his work on a similar agreement drawn up by a co-worker.**

ELHC: That's never going to work – that guy's work is too careless. If only it was that simple, there'd be no problem.

O: **He says 'If only it was that sim...', but doesn't finish his sentence.**

LHC: It is as simple as that. Now shut up and get on with it, I've got work to do.

O: **I say that it is that simple and tell him to get that specific agreement from his co-worker. He turns around and says nothing.**

ELHC: This really is pointless. He's only going to say that I've got it wrong and then I'll just have to start over again. Why can't he see that I need more time to deliver good work?

O: **He turns around and says nothing.**

LHC: What are you doing just standing there? Do it so I can get on with my work.

O: **I get impatient as nothing is happening. I tell him that it'll be fine and he can ask his co-worker for help if he has any trouble.**

LHC: Ok, problem solved, right?

ELHC: If he's going to be like this, then there's no point arguing. He's never going to change his mind.

O: **I ask him to print out the agreement and have it on my desk by the end of the afternoon so I can take it with me on Monday.**

ELHC: HHHhhhhuh. What an arrogant idiot.

O: **He walks out of the door without saying anything, but lets out a sigh.**

LHC: Loser! Now I'm annoyed again. Grr!

Session 16, week 4 – dialogue window

Hi Marcel,

Wow, that really was an eye-opener!

The results of this assignment were not what I had expected. It was surprisingly easy to fill in my employee's left-hand column in hindsight, but at the time, this was not what was going through my head. When I look back on it, it would seem that he was scared of making mistakes. To work more carefully, he needs more time. His work is usually flawless, which is exactly why I picked him to do this task. I didn't say any of this as he was so hesitant when he came into the office and this annoyed me. I was swamped with work and I didn't really give him a chance to get his side of the story across. My demeanour probably wasn't particularly warm or inviting either.

I see that I need to work on this!

Regards,
Peter

Session 17, week 5 – dialogue window

Hi Peter,

These are great insights you are gaining into yourself! You say that you need to work on these issues. What exactly would you like to change?

Let's review this conversation one last time – there's another assignment for you in the assignments window.

I look forward to reading your answer!

Regards,
Marcel
(ABC model: Internalize stage – action)

Explanation: the coach mirrors the client's informal greeting. This signifies that the social distance is reducing and the relationship is getting closer.

The coach uses linguistic strategy 12: Involve both yourself and your client in the activity. By talking in terms of 'us' instead of 'you', he includes himself in the task ahead. This helps reinforce the solidarity.

Session 17, week 5 – assignment window

Imagine the conversation that you have examined is an example of the 5 out of 10 score that you recently awarded yourself. Rewrite the conversation in the way you think it would have gone if you had been aware of the information in the left-hand column. How would a 7 out of 10 conversation go?

Explanation: this is an example of the solution-oriented technique.

Session 18, week 5 – dialogue window

Hi Marcel!

What I'd really like to change is how quickly I get irritated. I'd also like my conversations to run smoother. I spent ages trying to work out how to adapt the conversation, because I just couldn't make my left-hand column fit with positive reactions. However, I eventually realized that when you react differently, the left-hand column automatically changes to fit the responses. After all, the left-hand column is simply a reaction to the right-hand column!

I'm interested to know what you think of my adjusted conversation.

Regards,
Peter

Session 18, week 5 – worksheet window

O = Original
OLHC = Original left-hand column
ND = New dialogue
NED = New employee dialogue
NLHC = New left-hand column

O: He says he doesn't have enough information to make the necessary changes to the client's agreement.

OLCH: Oh no, there he goes again. Why do you always make such a fuss about things? You get paid extremely well for your work. Just do it!

ND: I tell him that I asked him specifically because his work is so accurate and the agreement is so important.

NED: He says that he wants to provide accurate work, and the lack of information means he'll need more time.

NLHC: There's always something, isn't there. I want this dealt with quickly.

ND: I say that it is urgent and ask him whether it would help to use a similar agreement drawn up by one of his colleagues to guide him.

NED: He says that this will only work if they are very similar.

NLHC: Ok, but we won't find that out by just standing here talking, will we?

ND: I say that we should be positive about it. Explain to your colleagues what the problem is and ask them if they have any similar agreements.

NED: He turns around and asks what we will do if they haven't.

NLHC: What if, what if... Just go and ask them so I can get back to work.

ND: I tell him to ask his co-workers first, and if they don't have any then we'll figure something else out.

NED: He nods.

NLHC: Ok, problem solved, right?

ND: I ask him to try and have the agreement on my desk by the end of the afternoon so I can take it with me on Monday.

NED: He says he will do his best and leaves the room.

Session 19, week 5 – dialogue window

Hi Peter!

Excellent and insightful work as usual – keep it up! You are right, the left-hand column automatically changes when the right-hand column (i.e. the conversation) runs differently. Good to see that you are trying to include more of your left-hand column in the conversation. This gives more clarity to the other person.

Now we've rehearsed these conversations on paper, it's time to put everything into practice. I've set you another assignment, although this one may take longer than the others. Do you think you could complete it by Wednesday?

Best of luck and have a good weekend!

Regards,
Marcel

(ABC model: Internalize stage – action)

Explanation: again, the coach starts with a compliment and explains what is positive about the behaviour. The coach is acknowledging the client's behaviour using positive reinforcement: this is an important factor in learning new behaviour.

Session 19, week 5 – assignment window

Assignment

During two conversations with employees, pay attention to what is in your left-hand column and how it affects the dialogue. Write down your experiences in the worksheet section. If you don't have time to do this straight after the conversation, then try to make brief notes to help you remember these new insights.

Explanation: here, the coach encourages the client to take the next step and apply his new insights in practice. The scale of the assignment is limited as baby steps result in greater success and quicker behavioural change. This makes it easier for the client to write quick reports and helps maintain the pace of the coaching process.

Supplement to session 19, week 5 – short text message (SMS)

Hi Peter! Good luck with the two conversations this week! Best wishes, Marcel.

Explanation: to show his involvement and give the client extra motivation, the coach sends a mobile text message (SMS). In the text message, the coach employs linguistic strategy 9: Confirm or assume knowledge of and attentiveness for your client's needs.

Session 20, week 6 – dialogue window

Hi Marcel,

I don't think I'll ever forget the left-hand column again! On Sunday, I went for a walk in the woods with my son. He wanted to climb up onto a tree stump, and I began to tell him to come back. I then immediately realized that in my left-hand column, it said 'because you'll get dirty'. Once I recognized this, I realized that it didn't matter if he got dirty. Though I don't think his mum's left-hand column would have said the same… :-)

I'm starting to notice what I think when I'm talking, although it's still difficult to bring it into the conversation and reflect it in your actions. In my first conversation with an employee, it went wrong. However, in the second, I did better.

I think I'll have to practice a lot more before I'm truly in sync with myself! :-)

Regards,
Peter

Session 20, week 6 – worksheet window

Conversation with employee 1

Steve is off sick. I call him to ask when he thinks he will be back. This is the third time in the last six months that he has called in sick. Because he plays an important part in preparing the work we do, his absence always puts us behind schedule. In hindsight, I realize that in my left-hand column was 'Sick? More like sick of work' and 'Great. Now we're going to fall massively behind.' I therefore didn't bother to ask him how he was, I just pushed him to get back to work as soon as possible.

Conversation with employee 2

Faye comes into my office with an agreement. I'm busy with an interim assessment of another employee. I notice that 'Oh no, I don't have time for this...' appears in my left-hand column. I ask her what I can do for her. She says she has a question about an agreement. I notice that I really don't want this to take long. I therefore ask her in a neutral tone if she can make it quick. As requested, she makes her question brief, and I notice my relief when I realize I know the answer off the top of my head. With her question answered, she leaves and I am free to continue with the employee assessment.

Session 21, week 6 – dialogue window

Hello again Peter,

I'm impressed with how quickly you are making progress! It's wonderful that you shared that story about your son. Was there a lot of washing to do? ;-) What exactly did you say when you realized what was in your left-hand column?

It's also impressive that you kept your cool and asked Faye to be brief instead of expressing your irritation at being disturbed. And you're right, if you want to be good at something, you have to keep trying. Practice makes perfect! I would therefore encourage you to practice this as much as possible and to pay attention to how the other person reacts. In the assignments section, you can find another assignment and in the library section, you can find a file containing a number of tips about being a better listener.

Enjoy practicing! I look forward to hearing what you discover.

Regards,
Marcel

(ABC model: Internalize stage – action)

Explanation: the client shares a personal moment, which the coach acknowledges using an expressive ('It's wonderful'). He also combines this with a question to facilitate awareness.

Session 21, week 6 – assignment window

Over the next few days, pay continual attention to what appears in your left-hand column and the effect it has on the dialogue. Make a note of what works well and what doesn't. Focus on the effect that each action has on the other person. Listen to them with both your eyes and ears:

Are they tense or relaxed?

Is their tone friendly or unfriendly?

Do they keep repeating their own viewpoint or do they appear to have taken on what you are saying?

For some tips on this, read the information about the seven levels of listening. You can find this file in the library section.

In the worksheet section, write down your experiences from the conversations.

Session 21, week 6 – library window

Listening is a skill that can be learned. Listening properly is not as simple as it might sound. In the following table, you can find an explanation of the seven levels of listening, as defined at carrièretijger.nl. You can then work out the level at which you generally listen to people. We also provide a number of tips to improve your listening skills.

The seven levels of listening

Level	Behaviour
7	Is sensitive to the needs of others and has time for people, asks for clarification, gives feedback, shows involvement.
6	Knows how to get people talking, exchanges information, listens to others and gives relaxed responses, asks questions to get to the heart of the matter.
5	Is always willing to take time to listen, comes across as interested and gives relevant feedback.
4	Lets others talk and asks for explanations, but prefers to keep the conversations strictly business.
3	Listens to others, is polite and obeys standard conversation etiquette, doesn't actively encourage the other person to talk, is mainly a reactive conversation partner.
2	Can restrain him/herself enough to listen to others albeit with visible impatience, prefers to talk about their own experiences.
1	Continually interrupts people, only wants to hear him/herself talking, is impatient when listening, can be irritable, doesn't really get to the point.

Listening – how to do it:

- Give the other person space to express themselves. Don't force them to talk.
- Maintain contact: look the other person in the eye (if culturally appropriate), nod, make affirmative sounds.
- People believe you are a good listener if the issues they believe to be important are reflected in your words.
- Summarize what the other person says.
- Indicate which points the other person made you think are most important.
- Ask if you have understood them correctly.
- Go into detail about what the other person said. Show interest in what they have to say.

Good listening skills particularly become noticeable in the follow-up to a conversation. Show that you have included the other person's comments, ideas and/or arguments in your account, plan or policy.

Listening attitude

What is the basic attitude that people assume at the start of a conversation? All too often, people see conversations as competitions, as discussions that need to be won by giving the best arguments. People want to show that they are intelligent and possess a lot of knowledge.

You should take a different approach: see every conversation as an opportunity to learn more about other people's opinions and perspectives. Be curious. Share ideas and gain wisdom. Involve yourself in what the other person is saying. Allow yourself to be influenced by the other people in the conversation and try to arrive at a mutual consensus.

Often, people listen with a presupposed idea or goal: they assume they already know what the speaker is about to say and they have already made their judgment. What about you? Do you start conversations with an open mind? Try to let go of your prejudices and expectations, reserve judgment and open yourself up to the speaker's message.

Supplement to session 21, week 6 – text message

Hi Peter! Good luck with your listening practice this week! Best wishes, Marcel.

Explanation: to give the client extra motivation, the coach sends a text message via Pluform's text message function. In the text message, the coach employs linguistic strategy 9: Confirm or assume knowledge of and attentiveness for your client's needs.

Session 22, week 7 – e-mail

Hi Marcel,

I'm afraid I didn't get round to writing about my experiences yet. I'll have time again tomorrow afternoon, so I can do it then. Is that ok?

Have a good evening,

Regards,
Peter

Explanation: the client needs more time to complete the assignment. He reports this via the internal e-mail system to ensure the coaching dialogue remains uncluttered.

Session 23, week 7 – e-mail

Hi Peter,

Sure, that's fine. Thanks for letting me know, and good luck with the assignment!

'Speak' to you tomorrow. :)

Regards,
Marcel

Session 24, week 7 – dialogue window

Hi Marcel,

Yeah, the next laundry day was definitely a busy one! Once I realized what my thought processes were in the conversation with my son, I let him go and climbed up onto the tree stump with him, pretending that it was a boat! The stump was covered in mud, and pretty soon, so were we! :) Once I saw the big smile on his face, I realized that there are more important things in life than the things that pop up in your left-hand column. I'm now trying to transfer this attitude to the communication with my employees.

I have documented my experiences in the worksheet section.

Regards,
Peter

Explanation: the client has made an important realization. This new awareness has resulted in a change in the client's behaviour.

Session 24, week 7 – worksheet window

When I compare my attitude to the descriptions in the listening-levels document, I find that I am usually at level 3, maybe even as low as 2. I would like to improve that to level 5. In order to do this, I have done my best to listen more to what the other person is saying. I'm doing quite well at the moment, especially with people who stick to the point and don't go on too long. And just as the document promised, I did start to learn things that I would otherwise have missed. For example, I learned something new from an employee about drawing up agreements.

I also managed to ask a fellow manager what exactly he wanted from me after he had given a rather long-winded and unclear explanation. I noticed that I was often thinking 'What exactly do you mean', and this time I managed to express this thought without sounding irritable!

When I know what the aim is, I find it easier to listen. However, I still have difficulty with long-winded stories. When somebody starts to go on and on, I start internally moaning again and have difficulty keeping my patience and maintaining an open mind. When this happened, I thought about the situation with my son and tried to delay my judgment.

I have also noticed that there is a definite link between my patience levels and my workload. At the moment, I am very busy and any dialogue can be disruptive. Of course, that's not my employees' fault, but it still gets to me. On Friday afternoon, for the first time in weeks, the workload eased off and I had more time on my hands. I immediately noticed that it was much easier to control my irritability when talking to an employee who always rambles on and on.

I will therefore see if I can do anything to ease my workload.

Session 25, week 7 – dialogue window

Hi Peter,

Wow, your assignment shows you are gaining a wealth of insight and self-awareness! You really are working hard.

As I understand, you have had the following realizations and breakthroughs:

There are more important things than what initially appears in your left-hand column (you can thank your son for that!)
You want to achieve listening level 5 (always willing to take time to listen, comes across as interested and gives relevant feedback).
Listening properly to other people helps you gain new information.
It is easier to listen when you know what the purpose is.
You have difficulty maintaining your patience when people talk for too long because you start grumbling in your head.
A heavy workload causes you to be more irritable in conversations.

What do you think you can do with this information?

Regards,
Marcel

(ABC model: Internalize stage – reflection)

Session 26, week 7 – dialogue window

Hi Marcel!

Thanks for the summary – it does help to have a point-by-point list of my new insights. I have already arranged a meeting with my supervisor to discuss what we can do about the heavy workload I have at the moment. Now I know that my workload has a direct influence on my patience levels, I can give my boss a more targeted explanation of what the problem is.

I also have a clear picture of what I have to do: make time for people, ensure that I know straight away what the conversation is about, and pay attention to what appears in my left-hand column.

I do still have difficulty with long-winded speakers. If you have any tips for dealing with this, then they'd be much appreciated!

Have a good weekend!

Regards,
Peter

Explanation: an example of an assertive. The client indicates what insights he has gained and that they have been put into action.

This is an example of a directive: the client (indirectly) asks for a tip from the coach. This affects the behaviour of the coach, who responds to the client's request.

Session 27, week 7 – dialogue window

Hi Peter!

Another crystal clear summary on your part! You've obviously gained a huge amount of useful insight.

About the tips for dealing with long-winded speakers: actually, you seem to have already worked out for yourself how to do this. After all, you wrote that when talking to a fellow manager who talks too much, you stepped in and asked him what he wanted from you. Asking questions helps the other person to get straight to the point and gives you a more active role in the conversation. It also allows you to test whether you have understood what the other person has said so far. The person then feels you are truly interested in what they have to say, which increases the quality and effectiveness of the conversation. My tip is therefore to keep asking questions!

In the library section, you will find information about different ways to ask questions. Use this information and your newly gained insights during conversations with your employees. I would then like you to write a report of these experiences in the worksheet section. Could you do that within the next couple of days?

By the way, how did the meeting with your boss go? Has your workload got any easier?

Best of luck!

Regards,
Marcel

(ABC model: Internalize stage – reflection combined with action)

Session 27, week 7 – library window

Asking questions
There are many different types of questions. For a detailed description of them all, visit http://en.wikipedia.org/wiki/Question.

In general, we use three different types of question: open, closed and multiple choice. The type you use depends on the objective of the conversation.

Open-ended questions
When you want to gain as much information as possible, it is best to use an open question. These often begin with the words, who, what, when, where, how or which. By asking an open question, you give the other person space to formulate the answer in whatever way they choose.

Example: Where are you going on holiday?
Answer: I'm planning to go to Germany, although if the weather is bad, I'll go to Spain.

Closed-ended questions
When you want a specific answer without background information, a closed question is your best option. These can only be answered with yes or no. The other person therefore doesn't have much room for manoeuvre in their answer. Closed-ended questions generally begin with auxiliary verbs (have, be, will, could etc.):

Example: Are you going on vacation to France?
Answer: No.
Or: Are you going on vacation to France or not?
Answer: No, I'm not.

There is another type of closed-ended question that does not begin with a verb. This type contains an assumption or judgment by the questioner. This type is therefore known as a suggestive question. It often contains an intonation to elicit an answer from the respondent.

Example: I guess you're going to France again on vacation?
Answer: No, why would you think that?

Multiple choice questions

If you want information about a particular option, you can ask a multiple choice question. These provide the respondent with a range of possible options to choose from.

Example: Are you going on vacation to France or Germany?
Answer: Germany.

Questions are most effective when you know beforehand what you do and do not want to hear. Asking questions and listening go hand in hand. When you listen carefully to the other person, it is easier to select questions that will elicit the response you want. Of course, this doesn't necessarily mean you have to agree with what is said!

Session 28, week 8 – dialogue window

Hi Marcel,

Asking questions is definitely a useful tool. I notice that I tend to ask closed-ended questions, and they are often very suggestive too. :-S I'm now practicing hard at asking more open-ended questions and using the right tone. Judging by the reactions from the people I talk to, my to-the-point demeanour can often make me seem blunt. Oh well, practice makes perfect!

   ;-)

However, I have noticed that my interpersonal contact is running much more smoothly than before. If I keep at it, I'm sure that my employee-satisfaction rating will go up. That would be wonderful!

My boss has agreed to lessen my workload by giving one of my tasks to a colleague. This has freed up around 2–3 extra hours per week. He also mentioned that he thought my interpersonal contact has improved!

Regards,
Peter

Explanation: this is an example of an assertive. The client indicates that he has learned something, and the coach will positively reinforce this by paying the client a compliment.

Session 28, week 8 – worksheet window

Gary comes to see me about arranging days off. He wants to take two weeks off, but he knows it's too busy to do that. So he starts talking about what he wants to do and how important to him it is. I say 'you'll need more than a week to do that, won't you?'. While I am saying it, I realize that this is a prime example of a suggestive question. He hesitantly says 'no, probably not'. I recover the situation and ask 'How many days off do you need?', and then 'How can we make sure you don't get behind on your work while you're away?'

Andy has made a mistake in his calculations, and starts to give reasons for the mistake. I say I don't want to know how it happened, I just want to know how to solve it. However, it comes across quite bluntly, and he looks down with a very guilty expression. I change to a friendlier tone and ask 'Ok, don't worry about it. Now what can we do to solve this problem?'

Daphne comes into my office with a charity collection box. I ask her how much she has collected so far. I also ask her about the charity and why it is close to her heart. We then have an interesting conversation about her ambition to build an orphanage in Latin America. In the past, I wouldn't have asked her and hence I'd probably never have known what the collection was for.

Session 29, week 8 – dialogue window

Hi Peter,

Congratulations on some great work and insightful results – keep it up! You're starting to correct yourself when you think you've said something the wrong way and you are showing that you care about the other person's point of view. And it's great that your boss has noticed the difference too!

These conversations show that you have fully understood the two-column principle, the listening tips and the importance of asking questions. Keep this up during all of your interpersonal contact with both employees and clients. If you still have any doubt about how to handle particular conversations or how they should have gone, then it is helpful to write down what appeared in your left-hand column. You can also review the information in the assignments section and your work in the worksheet section.

With one more week of the program remaining, it is a good time to take stock. For this purpose, you will find another exercise in the assignments section. Is there anything in particular that you'd like to work on in this final week?

I look forward to your response!

Kind regards,
Marcel

(ABC model: Internalize stage – review)

Explanation: the coach has entered the third stage of the ABC model: Sustain. Is this what the client wanted to learn? How can he maintain it? What should the client do next?

Session 29, week 8 – assignment window

In the weeks gone by, you have worked on improving your interpersonal contact with employees and you have already noticed the difference. In the objectives section, fill in the score that you would now give yourself with regard to this skill and explain your score in the worksheet section.

Explanation: the client is asked to reassess his skills in relation to the coaching objective. In this way, he validates what he has learned. This is the first step in the third stage of the ABC model: Sustain.

Session 30, week 9 – dialogue window

Hi Marcel,

It's great to see just how much progress I've made with my interpersonal contact. I thought it'd be much longer before I could award myself 7 out of 10. I notice that my employees also react to me more positively and come to my office more. Although I'm still quite busy, I like it because it is a sign things are heading in the right direction. It's confirmation that I'm becoming more approachable.

I can't really think of anything specific that I'd like to focus on other than to continue practicing what I've learned over the course of the program. Do you have any suggestions?

Speak to you soon,

Regards,
Peter

Session 30, week 9 – objectives window

Score: 7/10

Session 30, week 9 – worksheet window

By paying attention to my left-hand column, I become more aware of what I truly think and feel. I am often impatient because I expect people to say or do what I want them to. Now I make the effort to listen to what people have to say and I gain a lot of useful information as a result. This makes me less impatient. If I notice that I feel irritated, then I try to express the reason for my irritation in a calm and neutral tone. This gives all parties more leeway to accommodate one another's viewpoints.

Session 31, week 9 – dialogue window

Hi Peter,

Congratulations on all of your achievements! You have shown an excellent ability to reflect on your actions and had the courage to try new things in real-life scenarios. I'm hugely impressed! And I'm clearly not the only one. The fact that your employees are more willing to come to your office is a great compliment that I'm sure you'd never have expected two months ago.

I think we can round off the coaching program now. You are committed to upholding the insights you have gained and you have a clear picture of what you want to do (make time for people, ask for clarity about the purpose of the conversation and continue to pay careful attention to what appears in your left-hand column).

I have set you a final assignment, which you can find in the assignments section.

I am -as ever- curious about your findings!!

Regards,
Marcel

(ABC model: Sustain stage – validation and maintenance)

Session 31, week 9 – assignment window

It's the end of the coaching program, so it's time to reap everything you've sown. Write a summary of what you have learned. What are the most important insights you have gained? What will you need to make these behavioural changes last? And who can help you do this?

Session 32, week 9 – dialogue window

Hi Marcel,

I had never expected to achieve so much in such a short time.

I only truly realized how far I've come when I reviewed everything in order to write the summary. It occurred to me that it'd be a good idea to do this on a regular basis. I think it might be useful to arrange a couple more sessions with you in about six weeks' time. Would this be possible?

Have a great weekend!

Regards,
Peter

Session 32, week 9 – worksheet window

What have I learned?

The two-column method works really well for me. I would never have believed that I'd be able to make such quick progress regarding communication with my employees. By listening to my own thoughts, I am able to curb my irritability more often, or at least avoid letting it show. I have also discovered that what you think is not always important to what you want to achieve, and can often be contradictory to it. By listening before making your judgment, I often learn new things that help me achieve better results. I therefore think it is vital to listen carefully, even if I do have difficulty maintaining my patience with people who talk too much but say too little. I will deal with this problem in the future by asking at an early stage what the purpose of the conversation is. This helps me become more involved in the conversation and makes it easier to focus my attention on it. I have also realized that my workload is heavier than I thought and that this has a negative effect on my patience.

In order to make my behavioural changes stick, I must keep practicing my listening skills, pay attention to my left-hand column and regularly review this coaching program.

I will also ask a fellow team manager and my boss to warn me if I start slipping back into old habits.

Session 33, week 9 – dialogue window

Hi Peter,

Nice summary! It's surprising how long the list of new insights is, isn't it? Well done for asking your colleague and boss to monitor your progress – that'll be extremely helpful.

I'm curious about what you think the next step should be! (Don't worry, this doesn't mean you have to do another assignment! ;))

Your suggestion to contact each other again in six weeks' time to see how you are getting on, sounds great to me. If you would like, I can offer you a coaching credit card. This card contains ten credits which you can exchange for coaching. One credit equals one coaching session. Would that work for you?

Enjoy the rest of your weekend!

Regards,
Marcel

(ABC model: Sustain stage – validation and maintenance)

Explanation: E-coaching is perfect for brief top-up sessions. By purchasing a coaching credit card, the client can decide for himself when he wants to contact the coach.

Session 34, week 10 – dialogue window

Hi Marcel,

The coaching card sounds like a good idea – I'll take one! Thanks for everything you've done during the program, you've really helped me. I expect my next step will be transferring these insights to my contact with clients. I would like to give my clients greater opportunity to express themselves so I can learn more about what motivates them. This will have a very positive effect on the services we provide. I'm sure the insights I've gained during the coaching will help me to achieve this. And if they don't work every time, then I'll be back with my coaching card!

Good luck with your future coaching!

Regards,
Peter

Session 35, week 10 – dialogue window

Hi Peter,

No problem – you're welcome! Thank you for all the effort you made, your openness to new ideas and your willingness to learn. Good luck with your customer relations and your employee satisfaction evaluation. Let me know how everything works out!

I'll send you a message in six weeks' time. Until then, keep it up! :)

Kind regards,
Marcel

(ABC model: Sustain stage – enact)

Session 36, week 10 – dialogue window

Hi Marcel,

Don't worry – when the results of the employee satisfaction survey come in, you'll be the first to know! ;)

I look forward to hearing from you in six weeks!

Regards,
Peter

LIST OF CONTRIBUTORS

In Chapter 7 'Experiences of e-coaches', you find the practical experiences of dozens of coaches with e-coaching. Because of their willingness of sharing their e-coaching experiences with us had the opportunity to write this chapter. We would like to specially thank the following coaches for their contribution:

Ellen Sontag
Jan Wognum
Marco Tieleman
Lidwien Kamp
Margreet Steenbrink
Ramona van der Linden
Linda Schaap
Marjo van Tol
Yvonne Breur-Huisman
Ruud Polet
Margje Duursma
Audrey Peters
Annemieke J.W.E. Kramer
Emilie Sax van der Weijden
Bouchra Khayati
Charlotte van den Wall Bake
Kiona Monas
Annette Lechner
René van Winden
Rita Vanelderen
Jingxiu Hu
Cynthia Williams

Odile Seebregts
Viola Majoie
Marike Dirkx
Judith den Haan
Marga Spaanjaars-van Gestel
Marcel Jansen
Keimpe Zandvliet
Judith Groenendijk
Willem Huisman
Chris Laarman
Tjalda Postma
Marjanne Peters
Khadija Charafi

REFERENCES

Part I: Introduction to the world of e-coaching

Alemi, F., Haack, M. R., Nemes, S., Aughburns, R., Sinkule, J. and Neuhauser, D. (2007) Therapeutic emails. *Substance Abuse Treatment, Prevention and Policy, 2*(1), 7. doi: 10.1186/1747-597X-2-7

Alexander, G. and Renshaw, B. (2008) *Super Coaching*. Random House.

Aoun, S., Osseiran-Moisson, R., Shahid, S., Howat, P. and O'Connor, M. (2012) Telephone lifestyle coaching: is it feasible as a behavioural change intervention for men?. *Journal of Health Psychology, 17*(2), 227–236. doi:10.1177/1359105311413480

Baldwin, T. T. and Ford, J. K. (1988) Transfer of training: A review and directions for future research. *Personnel Psychology, 41*(1), 63–105. doi: 10.1111/j.1744-6570.1988.tb00632.x

Baron, L. and Morin, L. (2009) The coach–coachee relationship in executive coaching: A field study. *Human Resource Development Quarterly, 20*(1), 85–106. doi: 10.1002/hrdq.20009

Barthel, C. (2008) *Psychotherapie und Internet* (Doctoral dissertation). Retrieved from: www-brs.ub.ruhr-uni-bochum.de/netahtml/HSS/Diss/BarthelChristoph/diss.pdf

Bateson, M., Nettle, D. and Roberts, G. (2006) Cues of being watched enhance cooperation in a real-world setting. *Biology Letters, 2*(3), 412–414. doi: 10.1098/rsbl.2006.0509

Beattie, D., Cunningham, S., Jones, R. and Zelenko, O. (2006) I use online so the counsellors can't hear me crying: creating design solutions for online counselling. *Media International Australia, Incorporating Culture and Policy*, (118), 43–52. Retrieved from http://eprints.qut.edu.au /4678/1/4678.pdf

Beck, K. (2006) *Computervermittelte Kommunikation im Internet*. Oldenbourg Verlag.

Blume, B. D., Ford, J. K., Baldwin, T. T. and Huang, J. L. (2010) Transfer of training: A meta-analytic review. *Journal of Management, 36*(4), 1065–1105. doi:10.1177/0149206309352880

Bordia, P. (1997) Face-to-face versus computer-mediated communication: A synthesis of the experimental literature. *Journal of Business Communication, 34*(1), 99–118. doi: 10.1177/002194369703400106

Boyce, L. A. and Hernez-Broome, G. (2010) E-coaching: Consideration of leadership coaching in a virtual environment, in: Clutterbuck, D. and Hussain, Z. *Virtual Coach, Virtual Mentor*. Charlotte, NC: Information Age Publishing, Inc.

Brock, V. G. (2012) *Sourcebook of Coaching History*. Retrieved from: www.amazon.co.uk/Sourcebook-Coaching-History-Vikki-Brock/dp/1469986655

Brown, P. and Levinson, S. (1987) *Politeness: Some Universals in Language Usage*. New York: Cambridge University Press.

Bunz, U. and Campbell, S. W. (2002, October) Accommodating politeness indicators in personal electronic mail messages. In *Association of Internet Researcher's 3rd Annual Conference Maastricht, The Netherlands, October* (pp. 13–16). Available at http://bunz.comm.fsu.edu/AoIR2002politeness.pdf

Cakir, H., Bichelmeyer, B. A. and Cagiltay, K. (2005) Effects of cultural differences on e-mail communication in multicultural environments. *Electronic Journal of Communication/La Revue Electronique de Communication*, *15*(1&2). Retrieved from: www.cios.org/EJCPUBLIC/015/1/01512.HTML

Christopherson, K. M. (2007) The positive and negative implications of anonymity in Internet social interactions: 'On the Internet, nobody knows you're a dog'. *Computers in Human Behavior*, *23*(6), 3038–3056. doi: 10.1016/j.chb.2006.09.001

Clutterbuck, D. (2010) Welcome to the world of virtual coaching and mentoring, in: Clutterbuck, D. and Hussain, Z. *Virtual Coach, Virtual Mentor*. Charlotte, NC: Information Age Publishing Inc.

Croes, C. (2010) *Anonimiteit in de online hulpverlening* (Doctoral dissertation). Retrieved from www.e-hulp.nl/media/scripties/Anonimiteit_in_de_onlinehulpverlening.pdf

De Haan, E., Culpin, V. and Curd, J. (2011) Executive coaching in practice: what determines helpfulness for clients of coaching? *Personnel Review*, *40*(1), 24–44. doi: 10.1108/0048348111195500

De Haan, E. and Duckworth, A. (2010) The holy grail of executive coaching: Discovering what really works. *The OMC Coach and Mentor Journal*. Retrieved from: www.ashridge.org.uk/Website/IC.nsf/wFARATT/The%20Holy%20Grail%20of%20Executive%20Coaching:%20discovering%20what%20really%20works/$file/TheHolyGrailOfExecutiveCoaching.pdf

Deci, E.L. and Ryan, R.M. (1985) *Intrinsic Motivation and Self Determination In Human Behaviour*. Plenum Press, New York.

Döring, N. (2003) Sozialpsychologie des Internet. Die Bedeutung des Internet für Kommunikationsprozesse, Identitäten und Gruppen.

Dürscheid, C. (2005) 5 E-Mail—verändert sie das Schreiben? *Websprache. net: Sprache und Kommunikation im Internet*, *10*, 85–97. Retrieved from www.mediensprache.net/archiv/pubs/3-11-018110-X.pdf

Dürscheid, C. and Brommer, S. (2009) Getippte Dialoge in neuen Medien. Sprachkritische Aspekte und linguistische Analysen. *Linguistik online*, *37*(1), 09. Retrieved from www.linguistik-online.de/37_09/duerscheidBrommer.html

Fogg, B.J. (2011) *Changing Behaviour and Changing Policies*. Available at: www.bjfogg.com/stanford.html

Geißler, H. (ed.) (2008) *E-Coaching*. Schneider-Verlag Hohengehren.

Gleick, J. (2011) The Information: A History. *A Theory, A Flood*. London: Fourth Estate.

Grant, A. M. (2001) Towards a psychology of coaching. Unpublished manuscript, Sydney. www.eugenetherapy.com/Integration%20of%20psychology%20and%20business%20coaching.pdf

Grice, H. P. (1975) *Logic and conversation*. Speech acts, 41–58.

Herring, S. C., Stein, D. and Virtanen, T. (eds) (2013) *Pragmatics of Computer-mediated Communication*, *94*. De Gruyter Mouton.

Huls, E. (2001) *Dilemma's in menselijke interactie*. Utrecht: LEMMA.

Kielholz, A. (2008) Online-Kommunikation. *Die Psychologie der neuen Medien für die Berufspraxis, Heidelberg*.

Knaevelsrud, C., Jager, J. and Maercker, A. (2004) Internet-psychotherapie: Wirksamkeit und besonderheiten der therapeutischen beziehung. *Verhaltenstherapie, 14*(3), 174–183. doi: 10.1159/000080913

Knatz, B. and Dodier, B. (2003) *Hilfe aus dem Netz: Theorie und Praxis der Beratung per E-mail, 164.* Klett-Cotta.

Lee, H. S. and Cohn, L. D. (2010) Assessing coping strategies by analysing expressive writing samples. *Stress and Health, 26*(3), 250–260. doi: 10.1002/smi.1293

McDaniel, S. H. (2003) E-mail communication as an adjunct to systemic psychotherapy. *Journal of Systemic Therapies, 22*(3), 4–13. doi: 10.1521/jyst.22.3.4.23355

Mallen, M. J., Vogel, D. L. and Rochlen, A. B. (2005) The practical aspects of online counseling ethics, training, technology and competency. *The Counseling Psychologist, 33*(6), 776–818. doi: 10.1177/0011000005278625

Marterer, J. J. (2006) *Sprache und Neue Medien: Analyse des Sprachgebrauchs in den Kommunikationsformen E-Mail und Chat* (Doctoral dissertation, Universitätsbibliothek Giessen). Retrieved from http://geb.uni- giessen.de/geb/volltexte/2006/3854/pdf/ MartererJulia-2006-11-30.pdf

Marx, G. T. (1999) What's in a name? Some reflections on the sociology of anonymity. *The Information Society, 15*(2), 99–112. doi: 10.1080/019722499128565

Maslow, A. H. (1943) A theory of human motivation. *Psychological review, 50*(4), 370–396. doi: 10.1037/h0054346

Mehrabian, A. and Wiener, M. (1967) Decoding of inconsistent communications. *Journal of Personality and Social Psychology, 6*(1), 109–114. doi: 10.1037/h0024532

Murdoch, J. W. and Connor-Greene, P. A. (2000) Enhancing therapeutic impact and therapeutic alliance through electronic mail homework assignments. *The Journal of Psychotherapy Practice and Research, 9*(4), 232–237. Retrieved from www.ncbi.nlm.nih.gov/pmc/articles/PMC3330606/

Murphy, L. J. and Mitchell, D. L. (1998) When writing helps to heal: E-mail as therapy. *British Journal of Guidance and Counselling, 26*(1), 21–32. doi: 10.1080/03069889800760031

Olivero, G., Bane, K. D. and Kopelman, R. E. (1997) Executive coaching as a transfer of training tool: Effects on productivity in a public agency. *Public Personnel Management, 26*(4), 461–469. Retrieved from https://global.factiva.com/ga/default.aspx

Orwell, G. (1949) *Nineteen eighty-four.* London: Secker and Warburg.

Passmore, J., Peterson, D. and Freire, T. (2012) *The Wiley-Blackwell Handbook of the Psychology of Coaching and Mentoring.* Chichester: John Wiley & Sons.

Pavey-Scherer, D. L. (2008) *The Effects of Online Coaching on Instructional Consultation Skill Development and Treatment Process Integrity* (Doctoral dissertation). Retrieved from http://drum.lib.umd.edu/handle/1903/8765

Pedersen, D. M. (1997) Psychological functions of privacy. *Journal of Environmental Psychology, 17*(2), 147–156. doi: 10.1006/jevp.1997.0049

Pennebaker, J. W. and Graybeal, A. (2001) Patterns of natural language use: Disclosure, personality, and social integration. *Current Directions in Psychological Science, 10*(3), 90–93. doi: 10.1111/1467-8721.00123

Pennebaker, J. W., Kiecolt-Glaser, J. K. and Glaser, R. (1988) Disclosure of traumas and immune function: health implications for psychotherapy. *Journal of Consulting and Clinical Psychology, 56*(2), 239–245. doi: 10.1037/0022-006X.56.2.239

Pennebaker, J. W. and Seagal, J. D. (1999) Forming a story: The health benefits of narrative. *Journal of Clinical Psychology, 55*(10), 1243–1254. doi: 10.1002/(SICI)1097-4679(199910)55:10%3C1243::AID-JCLP6 %3E3.0.CO;2-N

Rex, A. (2009) *Auf der Suche nach dem verlorenen Sinn: über den Nutzen des Schreibens als Instrument der Bewältigung von Traumata und Krisen, 4.* LIT Verlag Münster.

Ribbers, A. P. C. and Waringa, R. A. (2011) *E-coaching voor ervaren coaches*. Intern manuscript, eCoachPro, Tilburg.

Ribbers, A. P. C. and Waringa, R. A. (2012) *E-coaching voor professionals*. Intern manuscript, eCoachPro/Europees Instituut, Tilburg.

Richards, D. and Tangney, B. (2008) An informal online learning community for student mental health at university: a preliminary investigation. *British Journal of Guidance and Counselling, 36*(1), 81–97. doi: 10.1080/03069880701715671

Rochlen, A. B., Zack, J. S. and Speyer, C. (2004) Online therapy: Review of relevant definitions, debates, and current empirical support. *Journal of Clinical Psychology, 60*(3), 269–283. doi: 10.1002/jclp.10263

Ruwaard, J., Lange, A., Bouwman, M., Broeksteeg, J. and Schrieken, B. (2007) E Mailed standardized cognitive behavioural treatment of work related stress: A randomized controlled trial. *Cognitive Behaviour Therapy, 36*(3), 179–192. doi: 10.1080/16506070701381863

Searle, J. R. (1976) A classification of illocutionary acts. *Language in Society, 5*(1), 1–23. doi: 10.1017/S0047404500006837

Searle, J. R. (1975) Indirect speech acts. *Syntax and Semantics, 3*, 59–82.

Spence, G. B. (2007) GAS powered coaching: Goal Attainment Scaling and its use in coaching research and practice. *International Coaching Psychology Review, 2*(2), 155–167. Retrieved from http://taos.publishpath.com/Websites/taos/images/Resources Manuscripts/Stelter_2007_Coaching_-_Pers_and_soc_meaning-making.pdf#page=43

Stienen, B. and de Gelder, B. (2011) Fear detection and visual awareness in perceiving bodily expressions. *Emotion, 11*(5), 1182–1189. doi: 10.1037/a0024032

Tannen, D., Schiffrin, D. and Hamilton, H. E. (eds) (2003) *The Handbook of Discourse Analysis*. Oxford: Blackwell.

Teo, T. S., Lim, V. K. and Lai, R. Y. (1999) Intrinsic and extrinsic motivation in Internet usage. *Omega, 27*(1), 25–37. doi: 10.1016/S0305-0483(98)00028-0

Thurlow, C., Lengel, L. and Tomic, A. (2004) *Computer Mediated Communication*. London: Sage.

Vail, P. L. (2003) *E-mail Coaching of Instructional Consultation Skills: Through the Eyes of Coaches and Consultant-Trainees* (Doctoral dissertation). Retrieved from http://drum.lib.umd.edu/bitstream/1903/259/1/dissertation.pdf

Van Kessel, L. (2007) Coaching, a field for professional supervisors?. *Ljetopis socijalnog rada, 14*(2), 387–432. Retrieved from http://hrcak.srce.hr/index.php?show=clanak&id_clanak_jezik=22080

Visser, C. F. and Bodien, G. S. (2009) *Doen wat werkt: Oplossingsgericht werken, coachen en managen*. Van Duuren Management.

Walther, J. B. (1992) Interpersonal effects in computer-mediated interaction a relational perspective. *Communication Research, 19*(1), 52–90. doi:10.1177/009365092019001003

Walther, J. B. (2007) Selective self-presentation in computer-mediated communication: Hyperpersonal dimensions of technology, language, and cognition. *Computers in Human Behavior, 23*(5), 2538–2557. doi: 10.1016/j.chb.2006.05.002

Weinhardt, M. (2009) *E-Mail-Beratung: Eine explorative Studie zu einer neuen Hilfeform in der sozialen Arbeit*. Weisbaden: Springer.

Yuki, M., Maddux, W. W. and Masuda, T. (2007) Are the windows to the soul the same in the East and West? Cultural differences in using the eyes and mouth as cues to recognize emotions in Japan and the United States. *Journal of Experimental Social Psychology, 43*(2), 303–311. doi: 10.1016/j.jesp.2006.02.004

Zajonc, R. B. (1965) *Social Facilitation*. Research Center for Group Dynamics, Institute for Social Research. Ann Arbor: University of Michigan.

Zajonc, R. B. (1966) *Social Psychology: An Experimental Approach.* Belmont, CA: Wadsworth Publishing Company.

Other sources

Erasmus@work, Rotterdam School of Management: www.erim.eur.nl/research/centres/smart-business-networks/projects/erasmus-work/
Kluwer Media: http://kluwermedia.nl/uitgave/129/special-over-het-nieuwe-werken.
National Board for Certified Counselors, Inc. and Center for Credentialing and Education, Inc. (2001) *The Practice of Internet Counseling: 1–6.*
University Twente: www.utwente.nl/ctit/cfes/Nieuws/2010_11_SocialeRevolutie.doc

Part II: Working as an e-coach

Argyris, C. and Schon, D. A. (1974) *Theory in Practice: Increasing Professional Effectiveness.* Oxford: Jossey-Bass.
Brown, P. and Levinson, S. (1987) *Politeness: Some Universals in Language Usage.* New York, NY: Cambridge University Press Droste, J. (2003) Het kiezen van een elektronische leeromgeving's-Hertogenbosch: CINOP.
Grice, H. P. (1975) *Logic and Conversation.* Speech acts, 41–58.
Herring, S. C., Stein, D. and Virtanen, T. (eds) (2013) *Pragmatics of Computer-mediated Communication, 94.* De Gruyter Mouton.
Huls, E. (2001) *Dilemma's in menselijke interactie.* Utrecht: LEMMA.
Schumacher, S. (2011) What employees should know about electronic performance monitoring. *ESSAI, 8*(1), 138–144. Retrieved from http://dc.cod.edu/essai/vol8/iss1/38
Searle, J. R. (1976) A classification of illocutionary acts. *Language in Society, 5*(1), 1–23. doi: 10.1017/S0047404500006837
Searle, J. R. (1975) Indirect speech acts. *Syntax and Semantics, 3,* 59–82.
Pol, I. G. M. (2012) *Coachen als professie: Fundamenten voor begeleiding naar heelheid.* Den Haag: Boom Lemma uitgevers.
Verbiest, A. (2004) *Als ik jou toch niet had: De taal van complimenten.* Amsterdam: Contact.

Other sources

2012 agreement Global Coaching Study. International Coaching Federation. Available at www.coachfederation.org/coachingstudy2012
Association for Counselling and Therapy Online (ACTO): www.acto-uk.org
EMCC Code of Ethics. Available at www.emccouncil.org/src/ultimo/models/Download/4.pdf
ICF Code of Ethics. Available at http://coachfederation.org/about/ethics.aspx?ItemNumber=854

INDEX

17538207R00103

Printed in Great Britain
by Amazon